NEFYN:
The Story of an Ancient Gwynedd Town and Parish

NEFYN:

The Story of an Ancient Gwynedd Town and Parish

ROLAND BOND

First Published in 2008

© Roland Bond
© Photographs: Roland Bond

ISBN: 978-1-84524-124-7

Published by
Llygad Gwalch, Ysgubor Plas,
Llwyndyrys, Pwllheli, Gwynedd, Wales LL53 6NG.
Tel: 01758 740432
e-mail: llyfrau@carreg-gwalch.com
www.carreg-gwalch.com

This book is dedicated to the memory
of all the mariners of Nefyn parish
who spent their lives sailing the seas and oceans of the world,
and especially those who lost their lives whilst doing so.

ACKNOWEDGEMENTS

I am very grateful to the staff of the Gwynedd Archives Caernarfon for their valuable assistance and advice at all times and for the friendly way in which that help was given.

I am also extremely indebted to the late Mr. Richard John Hughes of Nefyn for so willingly sharing with me his wealth of knowledge about the area, its history and its people.

My sincere thanks are also due to Clare Smith who has produced the photographs which appear within these pages.

I wish to acknowledge and pay tribute to the work of all those mentioned in the bibliography, for without their earlier studies and research, the writing of this little book would not have been possible.

Finally, I would like to thank my wife, Enfys, for her endless patience, support and help during the preparation of this book.

CONTENTS

1. INTRODUCTION

Nefyn is a small but ancient town and parish, lying approximately midway along the north facing coast of Llŷn in the county of Gwynedd. Previously part of the old county of Caernarfonshire, the town is situated a few hundred yards inland, behind cliffs which stand about 90 feet above the sweep of a curving sandy bay stretching from Bodeilias Point at the north eastern end to the headland at Penrhyn Nefyn at the south western extremity. Tucked under the cliffs at Penrhyn Nefyn are several cottages and a stone-built pier.

Beyond Penrhyn Nefyn is the larger bay of Porth Dinllaen, also backed by cliffs. Both bays are protected from the prevailing westerly winds by a promontory called Penrhyn Porth Dinllaen, which stretches out to sea for over half a mile. Huddled under the cliffs at the western end of this bay are Porth Dinllaen Lifeboat Station and the hamlet of Porth Dinllaen, which consists of a collection of cottages, a stone-built pier and the Tŷ Coch Inn. Above the bay of Porth Dinllaen is the scattered village of Morfa Nefyn, which is part of the parish of Nefyn.

The town of Nefyn itself is sited on fairly level ground and is protected on the landward side by the considerably higher upland areas of Mynydd Gwylwyr, Mynydd Nefyn and Garn Boduan. The dwellings within the town are fairly well spread out. At the bottom of Stryd y Ffynnon ('well street'), is Penisa'r-dre, one of the earliest parts of the town, for here is the old St. Mary's church, the water mill and the site of the early medieval Celtic priory. Another ancient part is Stryd y Plas ('palace street', so named after a palace of the Welsh Princes, built here during the early Middle Ages), which leads from the cross roads in the centre (Y Groes) up to Y Fron on the lower slopes of the Mynydd ('the mountain'), where there is another cluster of dwellings. The area around Y Maes and Stryd Fawr (high street), at the top end of the town, leads to Holborn and Penbryn Holborn and is now the main route to Pwllheli. The road which leaves the town centre in a south westerly direction, and which was built up during the first half of the 20th century, runs through the village of Morfa Nefyn, Edern and finally to Aberdaron at the end of the peninsula. Nefyn parish is bounded on the north east by the parish of Pistyll, on the east by Boduan parish and on the south west by the parishes of Ceidio and Edern.

First established as a scattered settlement during the early medieval period, Nefyn became one of the largest and most important manors of the Princes of Gwynedd. Under the Welsh princes and later under the English crown it saw a steady rise as an important administrative and trading centre in Llŷn and a strategic stopping place on the pilgrim route to Ynys Enlli (Bardsey Island). But at the start of the 15th century Nefyn was completely destroyed by the men of Owain Glyndŵr. Gradually the settlement began to re-establish itself, its economy built once more upon a combination of fishing and farming and the coastal trade attracted to its port. But regeneration was slow and the town never again achieved its former importance within Llŷn or the shire. It soon became overshadowed by Pwllheli on the southern coast of Llŷn as the chief market town and port of the peninsula. However, during the 18th and 19th centuries Nefyn did establish itself as a notable centre for herring fishing, granite quarrying, shipbuilding, ship repairing, ship ownership and ship insurance, although the neighbouring settlement of Porth Dinllaen emerged as the dominant port along the northern coast of Llŷn. During the second half of the 19th century and the early 20th century the parish of Nefyn provided large numbers of sailors and sea captains to man the British merchant fleet. This coincided with the dramatic rise of Welsh Nonconformity. It was the Liberal Nonconformist sea captains and other emergent local middle classes, who wrested power in their communities away from the Tory Anglican landowners and quarry owners, and who brought about changes in the political, religious, educational and social scene locally. In the closing years of the 19th century Nefyn began to develop as an unspoilt holiday destination for city dwellers, but the whole area around Nefyn might have changed if 19th century attempts to make Porth Dinllaen the packet station for Ireland had been successful.

As will have been noted from the foregoing brief summary, during its long history Nefyn has experienced a great many changes, and over the centuries the folk of Nefyn have been forced to adapt to greatly changing circumstances. In seeking to provide a brief insight into Nefyn's story, this study has employed a thematic approach. Whilst the themes have been ordered with chronology in mind, each section covers a particular topic across several centuries. Whilst every attempt has been made to avoid non-essential duplication, nevertheless it has sometimes been necessary to refer in a later chapter, to matters that have already been dealt with in a previous section.

At the time of writing, no book exists which attempts to narrate the fascinating story of this little Llŷn town and parish from early times to the present day. However, it must be emphasised that this book is not intended to be an exhaustive and detailed history of Nefyn; it merely sets out to provide the reader with glimpses into important aspects of Nefyn's story, thus affording an understanding of some of the factors and influences which have helped to shape Nefyn historically and make it what it is today. It is hoped that this book may shed some light for the reader upon the significance of certain Nefyn names and local features, thereby clarifying how they relate to the eventful story of this once important little place.

Although this book deals with the story of the town and the parish of Nefyn there are frequent references to places which lie just outside the parish. Such references are included because in earlier times the boundary of Nefyn extended further to the north east. Furthermore, other places like Porth Dinllaen, which lies within the neighbouring parish of Edern, are inextricably linked to Nefyn's story and therefore have had considerable impact upon the lives of Nefyn people.

In the preparation of this booklet the author has made considerable use of primary sources, although inevitably quite a lot of material has been gathered from a variety of works by other authors, as detailed in the bibliography. Whilst considerable care has been taken to avoid errors, the author accepts full responsibility for any misrepresentations of fact or inaccuracies of expression which may occur.

2. THE EARLY SETTLEMENT
OF THE NEFYN AREA

There is ample evidence that Llŷn has been settled since the Stone Age, for successive waves of inhabitants have left traces of their civilisation on the peninsula in the form of tools, weapons, pottery, standing stones, burial chambers, hill forts, early enclosures and hut systems, some of them within the immediate Nefyn area.

There have been 'finds' of Stone Age implements such as flints, arrow heads, stone axes and mace heads. The flints were probably left behind by primitive Mesolithic nomadic hunter-gatherers who penetrated the area from the west (about 8000 to 4000 BC) and who used flints on the end of their arrows and spears for hunting. Other artefacts discovered here were the stone tools left by tribes of Neolithic farmers, the first settled agricultural communities to inhabit the region from about 4000 BC to 2000 BC. For example, at Mynydd Rhiw, further down the peninsula, there is evidence of a Neolithic stone axe factory, dating from approximately 2500 BC to 2000 BC.

Subsequently, tribes of people made their way to Llŷn along western sea routes principally from the coasts of continental Europe. This was the Bronze Age which lasted from about 2000 BC to 800 BC. Examples of their pottery and implements have been unearthed within the area. Four urns and some miniature vessels were discovered within the parish of Nefyn, while Bronze Age tools and weapons have been found on Garn Fadrun, at Nant Gwrtheyrn, at Carnguwch (Pistyll) and at Tre'r Ceiri, a hillfort on Mynydd y Ceiri. Throughout Llŷn there are standing stones (many of indeterminate date but probably dating from the Neolithic and Bronze Ages), and these may have been either route markers to guide travellers or the remains of chambered tombs which have collapsed, leaving just one stone standing.

More extensive in Llŷn are the remains left by the Celtic-speaking peoples who came originally from central Europe, and the Celtic tribes from Ireland who arrived later. During what we now call the Iron Age (circa 800 BC to 100 AD), it was these folk who built the many hill forts to be found in the area around Nefyn. There is a bank and ditch type promontory fort on Penrhyn Dinllaen, and dry stone wall forts with clusters of dwellings on Garn Boduan, Garn Fadrun, Carreg y Llam and Tre'r Ceiri.

When the Romans invaded and ruled Britain, Llŷn was still inhabited by disparate tribes of Celtic speaking peoples. They had settled mainly on the upland areas and had refortified the Iron Age hill forts. The peninsula appears to have been left relatively undisturbed by the Romans. The nearest Roman garrison fort was Segontium (Caernarfon), and the Roman legions were struggling put down rebellions in eastern Britain and to ward off the northern Picts. For these reasons Llŷn was never fully colonised by Rome and it seems that the inhabitants of the peninsula were left alone to defend themselves against the warring tribes attacking Llŷn from Ireland.

In the Nefyn area, especially on the slopes of Mynydd Nefyn, there are examples of hut groups in enclosures, together with their associated field systems, as well as scattered huts with fields. Some of these are almost certainly of Roman date or from the post-Roman period but others may be pre-Roman in origin. These hut groups are the dwellings of settlers engaged in pastoral farming, who preferred to establish themselves on the higher pastures rather than on the coastal lowlands or the valley floors. There are also the remains of similar hut clusters and homesteads in the neighbouring parishes of Llanaelhaearn, Pistyll and Boduan.

During the period following the departure of the Romans in the second half of the 4th century, northern Wales was invaded by successive waves of foreign invaders, and some time later the Kingdom of Gwynedd began to emerge as a unified political entity. In the early 5th century a Brythonic chieftain, Cunedda, brought his tribe and warrior band from southern Scotland southwards to Wales. He was accepted as a strong unifying leader by the native inhabitants and his descendents were a long line of resilient and successful rulers. But for centuries northern Wales continued to repel attacks from all quarters – the Irish invading across the Irish Sea, the Saxons pushing westwards from England, the Vikings arriving in their longships to attack and plunder the coastal areas, and later the Norman Marcher lords invading northern Wales from the Welsh borders, especially from the lordship of Chester.

This period, known as the 'Dark Ages', was also the 'Age of Saints' when Christian missionaries arrived in Llŷn to establish religious cells and communities. Some sort of monastic cell or community was established at Nefyn and it is probable that a small settlement grew up around that early Celtic Christian 'llan' or enclosure. About 1860 a 7th century igneous standing stone, inscribed with a cross, stood on a mound (perhaps a burial mound since human bones were found nearby) near the parish boundary between Nefyn and Pistyll. This stone now serves as a doorway lintel in a cowshed at Ty'n y Cae Farm, Nefyn [1].

It is not possible to ascertain exactly when the first settlement appeared at Nefyn but early lowland settlers must have seen that this site was an eminently suitable one. Its position near the coast afforded easy communication by sea, and the sheltered, gently-shelving sandy beach beneath the cliffs was excellent for the launching and beaching of small boats; the site occupied reasonably level ground suitable for the growing of crops; the higher ground to the landward provided convenient grazing for animals; the seas offshore teemed with fish, especially during the annual visitation of the herring shoals, which provided an excellent source of nourishing food; and the site was well provided with water, for there were numerous springs, in addition to a small river which passed through the area on its way to the sea.

The earliest documentary reference to Nefyn dates from the second half of the 11th century, when Gruffydd ap Cynan, the Welsh Prince, sometimes landed in the bay of Nefyn whilst journeying in unfavourable weather conditions between northern Wales and Ireland. From his Irish base Gruffydd waged a long struggle against hostile tribal warbands and later the Normans to regain the land of his ancestors in northern Wales. His grandfather had been murdered while his father Cynan had been forced into exile across the Irish Sea. Several times Gruffydd ap Cynan was forced back to Ireland and, according to historical records, Llŷn was attacked by the Normans from the lordship of Chester, causing wholesale devastation. Finally, Gruffydd ap Cynan returned to Llŷn in 1098/9 to assume the overlordship of Gwynedd, and it was at Nefyn that he landed from a rowing boat to be welcomed by the people of Llŷn.

(1) *Royal Commission on Ancient and Historic Monuments in Wales, Caernarfonshire Vol. 3 –West.*

3. NEFYN, THE AGE OF SAINTS
AND THE PILGRIM WAY

The Romans established Christianity as the official religion in these islands, but the Celts who had settled in Llŷn were disparate bands of people who had not embraced the Christian faith. It was not until the early 5th century when Cunedda and his tribe, who had probably already come under Christian influence since his sons had Christian names, moved south from Scotland to settle this peninsula that some semblance of unity was achieved among the peoples in this region and that Christianity began to take root.

In the 5th and 6th centuries Christian missionaries, travelling from Gaul along the western sea routes, began to settle the coastal fringes of Britain, and Llŷn became one of the strongholds of Celtic Christianity in northern Wales. Attracted by its remoteness and comparative safety during these dangerous times, a number of religious leaders came to these parts to establish isolated cells and religious communities. These Celtic saints settled here, each establishing his 'llan' (plural – llannau), which was either an enclosed plot of land where an ascetic community of holy men lived in wattle and daub 'beehive' huts clustered around a small church, or an isolated spot where a religious hermit lived alone in his cell. Some followers of the original saints who settled here established their own 'llannau' in other places. This was the Age of Saints, and saints like Aelhaearn, Edern, Pedrog, Gwynhoedl, Ceidio, Cybi and Buan each established his own 'llan'. The lives of these early saints are shrouded in mystery and legend, but their memory lives on in the names of the places where they settled – Llanaelhaearn, Edern, Llanbedrog, Llangwnnadl, Ceidio, Llangybi and Boduan.

Perhaps the most famous local saint of all was St Beuno, who is most closely associated with Clynnog Fawr, where he founded an important religious settlement or 'clas' – a peculiarly Celtic phenomenon. The clas was a collection of monastic cells, from which saints went out on their missionary work. St Aelhaearn and St Edern are believed to have been followers of St Beuno. The chapel of St Beuno at Clynnog Church is one of 3 places in Llŷn where traditionally it is said that St Beuno is buried. For this reason it became a popular place of pilgrimage in its own right, and it was an important assembly point for pilgrims on their way to Ynys Enlli (Bardsey). At this time the Celtic Church in Wales was quite separate from the Church in Rome.

Other 'llannau' were dedicated, not to missionaries or religious

15

figures, but to wealthy and high status landowners who donated plots of land on which 'llannau' were established. Whilst the origin of Nefyn's name is uncertain, it has been suggested that the town may have taken its name originally from a Celtic saint. One view is that it may have been dedicated originally to Nyfain, the daughter of Brychan although certain authorities have questioned this. Subsequently, Nefyn was called Llanfair yn Nefyn (the Church of St Mary in Nefyn), perhaps an example of an early Celtic church dedication which was later abandoned in favour of the name of a Biblical saint. The old St Mary's church, rebuilt in 1827, still stands within its ancient raised churchyard at the lower end of the town, although it now houses a maritime museum.

According to tradition, in the late 5th century, St Cadfan came from Brittany to establish a religious community on Ynys Enlli. It is probable that by the end of the 6th century, Enlli was already a sanctuary for a community of devout men living lives of devotion and self denial. According to tradition, St Deiniol (founder of the monasteries at Bangor and Bangor Is-coed) was buried on Enlli and there is evidence that St Dyfrig, a bishop from southern Wales, was also buried there in the 6th century. In 1188 Gerald of Wales wrote that the bodies of a large number of holy men were buried there, and subsequently the island became known as the burial place of 20,000 saints.

Because of its reputation as a place of great sanctity, during the Middle Ages Enlli became an important place of pilgrimage. Large numbers of pilgrims came to Llŷn to tread the pilgrim way, and three pilgrimages to Ynys Enlli were considered equal to one visit to Rome. Pilgrims travelling from the north gathered at the 'clas' at Clynnog Fawr and then followed the northern route along the peninsula through Llanaelhaearn, over Yr Eifl to Pistyll and Nefyn. In each of these settlements there were houses, churches and religious communities, where pilgrims could pause to rest, pray and obtain food. On the route there was also a series of wells at which they could quench their thirst, and some of those ancient wells were considered to have miraculous healing powers.

Nefyn, situated midway along the northern coast of Llŷn, occupied a strategic place on the pilgrim route. By this time it was already an important settlement as well as the administrative and economic centre of the commote of Dinllaen. There was an ancient Celtic religious house, and it is believed that this priory was situated across the stream from St Mary's church, on the site now occupied by the children's playground. 'Tir y manach' ('monk's land') is mentioned in a title deed dated 1585, while on the 1838 Tithe Map parts of this land are referred to as Bryn Mynach ('monk's hill') and Cae Mynach ('monk's field'). Today Stryd y

Mynach ('monk street') is the name of the road which passes in front of the entrance to the churchyard.

Between 1155-6 and 1161-2 Cadwaladr ap Owain Gwynedd gifted to the Augustinian canons of Haughmond Abbey in Shropshire, Nefyn church and priory, together with certain lands in Nefyn. Subsequently, further grants of Nefyn land were made to Haughmond by other rulers. Those land gifts are detailed in the Haughmond charters thus: (1) the church at Nefyn together with "all the land between the two rivers where the church is situated and all the land of Cerniog." "And from the house of Griffri with meadowland all the way to the home of Waspitlillan". (2) three acres of land occupied by Gwion the cook. (3) "two parcels of land which the bald leper sometime held near Penodrayt" are referred to in one charter, while another document mentions "the lands held by Abraham the son of Aluredi the cobbler and the two sons of Serenna, namely Wasdewi and John his brother". These are probably different descriptions of the same two pieces of land and Penodrayt is clearly Penisa'r dre.

It was almost certainly at Nefyn priory that Archbishop Baldwin and Archdeacon Gerald Cambrensis spent the night before Palm Sunday in 1188 when they were touring Wales to preach support for the Third Crusade. Gerald records that in the priory he found a rare book which he had long been searching for – 'The prophecies of Merlin'. Prior William of Nefyn is mentioned in the Record of Caernarfon drawn up in 1252. But it seems that the priory had lapsed by 1342, for a charter of that year records that the masonry of its walls was being used for local house building.[1] Although the priory was defunct, the abbey at Haughmond retained title to Nefyn church until the dissolution of the abbey by Henry VIII in the 16th century. Both Nefyn priory and the town's well must have been welcome sights to many a leg-weary and thirsty medieval pilgrim!

From Nefyn the pilgrims followed the pilgrim way westwards through Edern, Tudweiliog, Penllech, Llangwnnadl and on to the end of the peninsula. Having reached Uwchmynydd and the headland at Braich y Pwll, they obtained their first view of the island. They gave thanks at St Mary's chapel for the journey completed thus far, prayed for a safe crossing to the island, and took a drink at St Mary's well. The site of the chapel remains unknown but the well now clings precariously to the cliffs at Braich y Pwll. Tradition would have us believe that they obtained sustenance at Aberdaron's Y Gegin Fawr ('the large kitchen') which now provides food for modern day tourists. The embarkation point for Enlli was the secluded cove at Porth Meudwy, south of Aberdaron, where the pilgrims boarded small rowing boats for the dangerous crossing of the

Sound, with its rapid tide race, treacherous currents, scattered rocks and strong whirlpools. One wonders how many of those devout medieval pilgrims lost their lives crossing that dangerous stretch of water. During the 13th century the Celtic monastery on Enlli became an Augustinian community until its dissolution in the 16th century. Today only the remains of its ruined walls are left.

During the later medieval period, pilgrimage was extremely popular and highly organised. Food and overnight accommodation were readily available and, as Nefyn was a natural stopping place midway along the route, the large numbers of pilgrims resting within the town must have brought much additional wealth and status to the place. As Professor T. Jones-Pierce has pointed out, pilgrimages must have given the whole region the air of a medieval holiday resort, and there is no doubt that Nefyn's development as one of the pre-eminent royal manors in Gwynedd was due in part to its important position on the pilgrim road to Enlli [2].

(1) Rees,'*The Cartulary of Haughmond Abbey*
(2) Jones-Pierce, *The Old Borough of Nefyn*

4. THE RISE AND FALL OF A
MEDIEVAL MANOR

A glance at a street plan of Nefyn reveals that it was essentially a native Welsh settlement, the physical layout of which had grown organically, unlike the planned Edwardian towns of Caernarfon and Conwy with their rectilinear street patterns. Prior to the Edwardian conquest, Nefyn was already a substantial and prosperous Welsh community. Under the house of Gwynedd, the kingdom was divided into cantrefs, which were subdivided for administrative purposes into smaller units called commotes, each commote consisting of several townships. The cantref of Llŷn was split into 3 commotes one of which was the commote of Dinllaen, and Nefyn emerged as the main township and commotal centre of Dinllaen. The bountiful supplies of herring which frequented its shores, together with its location at a strategic point on the pilgrim road, were instrumental in promoting the importance of this settlement. Early on, certain of its inhabitants were already looked upon as burgesses, for when Maredudd ap Cynan made his grant of land in Nefyn to Haughmond Abbey in the late 12th/early 13th century, two of the signatories were detailed as "Roberto et Stephano burgensibus de Nevin"[1].

In pre-Conquest Gwynedd Nefyn was not only the administrative centre of the commote, it was also the hub of its economic life and an important royal seat. It is clear that the Princes of Gwynedd did much to promote and regulate the economic fortunes of commotal centres like Nefyn, where they offered special trading concessions from which they profited financially.

It was under the two Llywelyns that Nefyn developed rapidly as the administrative and trading capital of the commote of Dinllaen and one of the chief urban centres in Gwynedd. At this time Nefyn was one of the largest manors of the Princes of Gwynedd. It possessed a splendid plas or royal residence, which was used by the Prince or his royal officials whenever they visited the town – hence one of the roads in Nefyn is still called Stryd y Plas. The importance of Nefyn at this time may be judged from the nature of this royal residence. It was a traditional timber, wattle and thatch Welsh hall-house, but far more elaborate in design than most, for it included a number of upper storey rooms overlooking the great hall, as well as several additional rooms not normally found in Welsh manor houses of the period[2]. Within the town there was also a castle, probably built in the late 12th century to afford protection at a time when the Norman Earl of Chester was pushing westwards. It was perhaps a motte and bailey castle and, although no evidence of a bailey exists now, the mutilated remains of the motte can still be seen at Pen y Bryn, surmounted by a 19th century stone watch tower. There is nothing to suggest that Nefyn itself was ever fortified with a defensive wall. As has already been mentioned, there was an ancient priory, and Nefyn was served by 3 mills, one in the town and two others within the manor. There was also a royal farm, consisting of a garden, meadows, extensive hill grazing and over 200 acres of arable land.

The death of Llywelyn ap Gruffudd in battle during December 1282 and the capture and execution of his brother, Dafydd, in June 1283, meant that the power of the princes of Gwynedd had been destroyed, and this very Welsh kingdom now belonged to an English king. In the summer of 1284 Edward I chose Nefyn as the venue for an elaborate tournament to celebrate his victory. This costly and ostentatious spectacle, based upon the idea of King Arthur's Round Table, was almost certainly staged on Cae Iorwerth ('Edward's field') and Cae Ymryson ('the field of the contest'). No expense was spared in staging this celebratory event, which was attended by the English nobility as well as a host of foreign dignitaries, and which was intended to emphasise that in Edward the people had a second King Arthur. The tournament fields can be reached by walking down Stryd y Plas as far as Capel Seion where, on the opposite side of the road, there is a footpath which runs along the back of several houses and gardens. That path leads into those low lying fields, one of which is also known locally as Cae Sgadan ('the herring field') because when photographed from above it resembles the shape of a fish.

During Edward I's reign, Nefyn developed rapidly. In 1284 there were 55 households in Nefyn, of which only 5 were bondmen (unfree peasants) tied to the land and the lord of the manor. They were obliged to give annual dues in kind to their lord and to perform a range of duties for him each year. The other 50 households were headed by freemen, who paid annual cash rents. Nefyn at this time was described as 'the borough of Nefyn' and, although no charter had been granted, the native freemen certainly considered themselves to be of similar status to the burgesses of an English market town. By 1293, less than 10 years later, the population had nearly doubled to 93 taxpayers, and these included half a dozen retail tradesmen, a goldsmith, an innkeeper and Madog the priest. About half the population owned fishing nets and/or boats, a clear indication that fishing was very important in the lives of these townsfolk. In addition, a weekly market was being held here and ships were calling regularly at the harbour to trade.

In 1349 the Black Prince granted the revenue from the manors of Nefyn and Pwllheli to Nigel de Loryng, who had fought alongside him at the Battle of Poitiers. In 1355 the Nefyn burgesses managed to obtain from the Black Prince a royal charter of privileges for the town. This charter confirmed the weekly market and granted the burgesses several important benefits, including the right to hold two annual two-day fairs. It also decreed that henceforth all the commote's trade was to be conducted within the borough at the aforesaid markets and fairs.

Therefore, in the first half of the 14th century, it is possible to visualise Nefyn as a prosperous and thriving agricultural community with a growing population, whose freemen were farming strips in the Open Fields, making use of the grazing on the higher land and fishing for herring during the season. It was the economic centre of this part of Llŷn, holding its two annual fairs and its weekly markets, and attracting a considerable amount of maritime trade.

A catastrophic change in the town's fortune occurred during the second half of the 14th century, brought about by the Black Death and the supporters of Owain Glyndŵr. It is estimated that in Britain as a whole, the 14th century plague outbreaks may have reduced the entire population by as much as a half by the end of the century, but detailed information about the Black Death in Nefyn is not available. The plague appears to have spread into Wales along trading routes, and it probably arrived in Caernarfonshire in the autumn of 1349. Llŷn, and especially the commote of Dinllaen, appears to have been one of the worst affected parts of the shire. Records for Dinllaen reveal that rents were not being collected at the end of 1349 (presumably because tenants had died) and lands remained untenanted as late as 1352. If the plague caused so many deaths in Dinllaen, it is inconceivable that Nefyn, the chief trading centre of the commote, would not have been severely affected by this scourge.

Even more disastrous for this town which had hosted Edward I's grand tournament and which had been granted a royal charter by an English prince, was the Glyndŵr uprising. Angered by Nefyn's associations with English royalty, the followers of Owain Glyndŵr were bound to exact revenge upon the town as they did with all other colonial and priviledged towns in Wales where the local Welsh were economically and racially second class citizens. In 1400 they descended upon Nefyn, attacked it and burned it to the ground, forcing all the inhabitants to flee. So thoroughly did they carry out their retribution that, 13 years later, the place was reported still to be uninhabited with no rents collected.

Eventually a settlement was re-established here, but accounts dating from the second half of the 15th century reveal that the borough was in a very poor economic state. Regeneration and growth proved to be so slow

21

that, even as late as the reign of Charles I in the 17th century, the economic condition of the borough was much the same as it had been at the time of Edward I 350 years earlier. Never again was Nefyn to achieve its former status as one of the principal administrative and economic centres in Gwynedd.

(1) The Cartulary of Haughmond Abbey, Deed No. 787.
(2)T. Pierce-Jones, *The Old Borough of Nefyn 1355-1882.*

5. THE LANDOWNING GENTRY AND THE CORPORATION OF NEFYN

The turbulent years of the Glyndŵr rising and the Wars of the Roses of the 15th century helped to accelerate the disintegration of the old Welsh tribal society. The dissolution of the monasteries and the disposal of their lands by Henry VIII meant that large tracts of former monastic land were now available for purchase from the Crown. By the end of the 16th century certain enterprising local families had begun to acquire these and other lands, accumulate wealth, build small country houses and achieve social pre-eminence. This was the new emergent Welsh uchwelyr or local landed gentry, and several such families had acquired lands and established themselves within the borough of Nefyn by the beginning of the 17th century. These were the families of Cefnamwlch, Madryn, Bodfel and Boduan.

These northern Wales *uchelwyr* families became the pillars of the establishment, serving in all manner of public offices and dispensing justice as Justices of the Peace. Later their sons went to English public schools, Oxford and Cambridge Universities and the London Law Schools. They served as officers in the army and navy, they became Members of Parliament and some achieved high office in the Government, the Judiciary and the Church.

Over time they increased their landholding through encroachment, inheritance, land purchase, enclosure, and by shrewdly marrying the heiresses to other landed estates. Some of them amassed huge estates which extended across several Welsh counties. These gentrified families split into factions along old tribal lines, vying with each other for political power and influence. Rival local landowners frequently resorted to litigation against one another.

In 17th century Nefyn the main protagonists were the well-established Griffiths family of Cefnamwlch and the Wynnes of Boduan, who were relative newcomers to the borough with a mere foothold here. In 1632, when Charles I sent Humphrey Jones, his Receiver-General, to Nefyn to reassert the Crown's rights to lands within the borough, Thomas Wynne of Boduan led the majority of burgesses in their opposition to the King's proposals, while John Griffith of Cefnamwlch led a minority who were prepared to accede to the King's demands. Subsequently it was claimed that Griffiths had been secretly negotiating to purchase the Nefyn lease from the Crown for himself, but Wynne, too, had aspired to acquire Nefyn, although each maintained that he had been acting in the best interests of the burgesses.

The Receiver-General met the burgesses in Nefyn churchyard where Thomas Wynne whipped up the passions of the assembled crowd to fever pitch, arguing that those holding property in Nefyn would fight to defend their lands 'foot by foot'. The mood of the meeting became so ugly that it almost degenerated into a riot and the Receiver was forced to beat a hasty retreat.

Thomas Wynne, whose influence in Nefyn was rather tenuous but who had a mansion and a substantial landholding in the neighbouring parish of Boduan, was determined to increase his family's power and standing locally within Llŷn and within the shire at large. First, he assumed the mayoralty of Nefyn and then established a relative by marriage as mayor of Pwllheli. These were the two most important urban centres in Llŷn. Having secured control of both mayoralties, he set about rigging the electoral roll of both boroughs by admitting large numbers of non-resident burgesses to them, mostly his Boduan tenants who would be sympathetic to his cause. From 1707 to 1713, as Mayor of Nefyn, Thomas Wynne admitted 689 new burgesses, most of them residing outside the borough. The same process was carried out at Pwllheli and, as a consequence, he won convincingly the 1713 Parliamentary Election for the Caernarfonshire boroughs. The Wynne family retained the mayoralty of Nefyn throughout the 18th century and during most of the 19th century. They also retained the parliamentary seat for the Caernarfonshire Boroughs until 1790. The manipulation of the Nefyn electoral roll continued throughout the 18th century and beyond, so that by 1836 it was reported that "there are 70 or 80 burgesses but not more than 15 are resident within the borough"[1].

In Nefyn this situation had a disastrous effect upon the processes of local government, which had deteriorated greatly since the 14th century. At the time of the 1355 Charter, all Nefyn burgesses lived within the borough, and the burgess body as a whole was responsible for administering all the borough's affairs, apart from dealing with serious criminal offences. At the courts leet, which met in May and at Michaelmas (September) each year, the burgesses elected their borough officials and a Grand Jury reported any infringements of the customs and regulations of the borough. In addition, a small court met monthly to resolve disputes between residents. Thus the resident burgesses of Nefyn had complete control of the affairs of the borough without interference from outsiders.

By the 18th century the situation was very different. The Nefyn Court Book (1756-82) reveals that, by this time, the Grand Jury was making very few presentments to the courts leet, and the May court had ceased to sit regularly. Much time at the courts leet was taken up with the admission of new burgesses, the majority of whom resided outside the borough. The small court met only spasmodically to deal with minor disputes, many of them of an extremely petty nature.

Thus the hereditary mayoralty and the manipulation of the burgess roll had impinged disastrously upon the 'corporation' and the administration of its affairs. A succession of hereditary mayors showed little real or sustained interest in local government matters. The factional nature of the burgess body, with non-residents greatly outnumbering residents, destroyed any semblance of public-spiritedness among the burgesses. Consequently those who held office within the corporation showed little appetite for performing their duties meaningfully. Although, from the 1830's onwards, local leaders revitalised to some extent the administration of municipal affairs within the town, by the 1880's Nefyn's population remained static and fairly modest. By now, this once pre-eminent Llŷn town had been overshadowed by Pwllheli as the most important town on the peninsula, and therefore had become relatively unimportant. It is not surprising that in 1882 Nefyn lost its borough status and reverted simply to a parish.

Today, Nefyn's association with the landowning gentry, such as Lord Newborough of Glynllifon and Boduan (Sir Thomas Wynn was created 1st Baron Newborough in 1776), the Edwards family of Nanhoron (who from the second half of the 18th century onwards had built up their land holding in Nefyn) and the Madryn family from Madryn Castle, are preserved in local names such as Tŷ Newborough (formerly a public house called the Newborough Arms), Glynllifon Terrace, the Nanhoron Arms, the Nanhoron Stores and Siop Madryn, while the name of Lord Newborough, as Mayor of Nefyn, is inscribed on the stone-built structure erected over the town's well in 1868.

Furthermore, it is interesting to note that two semi-detached cottages called Tŷ Receiver and Mursefer, situated at the bottom of Stryd y Ffynnon, were built in 1774-5 by Captain Timothy Edwards R.N. (a member of the Nanhoron family) on the site of an earlier dwelling once owned by Humphrey Jones of Craflwyn and Penrhyn, King Charles I's Receiver-General of Revenues for North Wales – hence the name Tŷ Receiver. This is the same Humphrey Jones who had tried to negotiate with the Nefyn burgesses in 1632 and who had been forced to flee their wrath during the meeting in Nefyn churchyard.

(1) Report on the Borough of Nefyn 1836

6. THE HERRING FISHING

As previously stated, since the early Middle Ages the seasonal herring fishing, combined with agriculture, had been the means by which the majority of Nefyn folk had gained their livelihood. For centuries most Nefyn men could reasonably be described as either tenant farmers who owned a share in fishing boats and nets, or as fishermen who reared animals and cultivated their plots of lands around their dwellings and their strips in the Open Fields. This is well illustrated by an early document which records that Einion ap Adda possessed 38 animals and 3 fishing nets; Ieuan ap Madog owned 6 animals, 1 boat and 4 nets; Llywarch Crun owned 1 animal and 1 net; Bleddyn Fychan had 11 animals, 1 boat and 3 nets; Tangwystal wraig Addaf possessed 4 animals and 1 net; while Dai Bach owned 3 animals and 2 nets. This inventory not only gives an insight into the dual nature of the occupations of Nefyn folk but also indicates the differing degrees of prosperity they enjoyed.

The Nefyn fishing industry developed greatly during the 18th century. In 1705, 1718, 1750 and 1787 a series of Bounty Acts were passed to promote the catching and export of herrings, and by 1748 a pier had been built at Porth Nefyn. Some herrings were consumed locally, while others were sold to local travelling fish merchants who resold them at a profit to their customers in inland villages and farms, to be eaten as fresh herrings. But the bulk of each catch was either salted (white herrings) or smoked (red herrings) in special curing houses, to be exported by the barrel to ports like Chester, Liverpool and Dublin. In 1771 the annual catch at Nefyn was valued at £4000, an enormous sum in those days. The store houses built along bay of Nefyn for processing the herrings, are mentioned in documents dated 1757, 1763, 1775-7 and 1825, and Hyde-Hall, writing in the early 19th century, speaks of the many curing houses along the shore of the bay at Nefyn. In 1757 6 pence per barrel was paid to salt 66 barrels of herrings in one of the Nefyn storehouses. There were about 40 fishing boats belonging to Nefyn during the first decade of the 19th century when Hyde-Hall visited the town.

According to Parry's *New Guide to Wales* (1846) the herrings caught off the northern coast of Llŷn were considered bigger and better than those found off the southern coast of the peninsula, and the exceptional quality of Nefyn herrings is evidenced by the traditional cry of the Nefyn herring sellers:-

Penwaig Nefyn, Penwaig Nefyn	*Nefyn herrings, Nefyn herrings*
Bolia fel tafarnwyr	*Bellies like innkeepers*
Cefna fel ffarmwrs.	*Backs like farmers.*

So famous were Nefyn herrings that in 1756 the town was referred to as "Nefyn the Fish" while locally the herring was often known as "Nefyn Beef".

At first Nefyn men built their own fishing boats upon the beach and these early boats were commonly the property of 7 persons, as Hyde-Hall observed. Later, Nefyn fishermen purchased commercially-built boats, especially those built by Matthews of Menai Bridge. These were double-ended boats which could easily be launched from and beached in the gently sloping sandy bay, whatever the state of the tide. They were 18 feet long with a 7 foot beam, huge 14 foot oars and a crew of 4 men. Three of the crew rowed while the fourth, usually the owner, steered. Each crew member normally provided 2 or 3 nets, and these were all joined together to form a long wall of netting, which was either secured by means of iron anchors or allowed to drift freely using large leather marker buoys. Cork floats were attached at intervals to the top of the netting and stone weights were secured to the bottom edge to enable the net to 'stand' upright below the surface of the water. Since herrings are pelagic fish which swim near the surface of the sea, they would swim into the net and become trapped by their gills in the 1 inch mesh. Usually a catch was shared 5 ways, one share being allocated to each crew member and one for the boat. At Nefyn the recognised herring fishing season extended from September to January.

Some Nefyn fishermen were full-timers, who from February to August fished for other types of fish. But most were part-timers who, outside the herring season, worked on the land, or were skilled craftsmen, quarry workers or mariners. Throughout the 19th century herring fishing remained important in Nefyn, although there were periods when the herrings were scarce. It was reported in 1836 that the herring fishing had failed for 6 or 7 years. At other times there was a glut of herrings, which on one occasion were piled up on the fields of Cae Rhyg and used as fertiliser. As late as 1910, there were still about 40 fishing boats operating from Nefyn.

By the 1920's Nefyn had ceased to be a herring port of any significance. The herrings were no longer to be found in large numbers off the Nefyn coast. The Nefyn coat of arms (3 silver herrings upon a shield), the stone look-out tower built in 1846 upon the old castle motte so that local inhabitants could watch for the fishing boats returning, the sign of 'The Three Herrings' (formerly the old Nanhoron Arms) at the top of Stryd y Ffynnon and Caffi'r Penwaig ('herring café') at Pen y Bryn are now the only visual reminders of this once flourishing and important Nefyn industry.

7. AGRICULTURE

As pointed out in the last section, since the Middle Ages the majority of Nefyn men had combined farming with fishing. They tended their garden plots, they grazed a few animals on the higher commons and waste lands, they cultivated their strips in the Open Fields, which lay to the west and south of the town (the path between the fields, leading from Penisa'r dre to the top of the cliffs, is still called 'Lleiniau', meaning strips) and during the herring season, they took to the boats with their nets. Herring fishing, combined with agriculture, was still the means by which many Nefyn men subsisted in the mid 18th century.

Grazing and livestock rearing had been the main occupations of Llŷn farmers for centuries. In the 17th century the production of store cattle for export was so important to the economy of Caernarfonshire that Archbishop John Williams once likened it to a Spanish treasure fleet bringing gold and silver to the area. Writing of Llŷn in 1773, Pennant mentioned that over 3000 black cattle were exported annually from these parts. Each year professional drovers purchased Welsh blacks from farms and fairs (such as the 2 annual Nefyn fairs) and drove them, along well-established cattle-drovers' routes in large herds to English cattle markets mainly in the Midlands and the London area. There they were sold to be fattened.

In the second half of the 18th century corn began to figure more prominently for Llŷn farmers. Writers visiting Nefyn in the late 18th and early 19th centuries spoke of the large quantities of agricultural produce exported through the ports of Nefyn and Porth Dinllaen, especially cereals, butter and cheese, hens and eggs, pigs and pig meat. Much of this produce was exported to the Liverpool markets.

During the 18th century there had been a revolution in agricultural methods, but the traditional system whereby the townsfolk held arable land in scattered strips and grazed animals upon the extensive commons and wastes was not conducive to the new improved ways of farming. The 1838 Nefyn Tithe Map reveals that there were still large numbers of strips in existence, and even as late as 1878, as the Nanhoron Rental for Nefyn shows, some cottagers were still cultivating their strips or quillets. Pennant observed in 1773 that "the country is in an unimproved state...."[1], while William Williams of Llandygai stated in 1805 that almost two thirds of the land in Llŷn was in "a state of nature, remaining heathy or gorsey wastes, tho' the soil in most of these wastes is of a productive quality and excellent in kind"[2]. Hyde-Hall writing of Nefyn in 1809-11 wrote, "Of agriculture no favourable account can be given", alluding to the "slovenly management of the fields", "the ragged banks of earth" in place of fences, the lack of trees and "the bareness of the parish"[3]. Pennant maintained that the agriculture was in a poor state because it was neglected for the sake of the herring fishing, although Hyde-Hall refuted this suggestion, arguing that the harvest from the land was "always either housed, or at least saved, before the coming of the fish."[4]

Despite these hindrances to agricultural change at the beginning of the 19th century, the landed gentry were making some efforts to bring about improvements. Pennant spoke of "the laudable example of the gentry"[5], and landowners such as the Edwards family of Nanhoron, who by this time had become one of the chief landowners in Nefyn, were pioneers in agricultural and estate improvement. Furthermore, by the early 19th century Richard Edwards of Nanhoron, Lord Newborough of Glynllifon, Mr Jones Parry of Madryn Castle and Sir Robert Williams Vaughan of Hengwrt near Dolgellau were exchanging strips in Nefyn in order to consolidate their holdings into larger tracts of land. Nevertheless, despite such efforts, William Williams of Llandygai criticised the local gentleman landowners for racking up the rents of their tenants and for failing to offer them proper leases, an insecurity of tenure which discouraged improvement to farms and small holdings.

The late 18th and early 19th centuries saw the wholesale enclosure of land across England and Wales, for there was a need to make more productive use of much of it as William Williams had advocated. He saw enclosure of the wastes as a necessary improvement but was anxious that the ordinary folk should not be injured in the process. He argued that those dispossessed of their homes built on encroachments at the edges of the wastes ought to be fully compensated. Moreover, he maintained that if many of the wastes were enclosed, there was no need to enclose the commons which were vital for the ordinary folk. His advice went unheeded. In 1812 an Act of Parliament was passed enclosing over 6500 acres of waste and commons in Nefyn, Pistyll, Carnguwch, Llanaelhaearn, Clynnog and Llanllyfni. As a result, not only were the manorial commons taken away in Nefyn but the borough also lost 300-400 acres of municipal common, because the officers of the corporation did not have sufficient skill and knowledge to deal properly in this matter. As the 1836 Nefyn Report states, the solicitor and agent making the necessary arrangements for enclosure, "sent for the bailiffs and made them sign away their common. They were not scholars and they were tricked into signing".[6]

Although enclosure did extend the margins of cultivation and resulted in agricultural improvements, the motives of the wealthy landowners who profited from it were far from altruistic. They saw enclosure as a means of increasing their landholding and thus enhancing their wealth, status and influence. Two of the main beneficiaries of enclosure in Nefyn were Lord Newborough of Glynllifon and Richard Edwards of Nanhoron. If enclosure benefited the local gentry, it had very substantial economic and social consequences for the ordinary folk of the town and parish. The Nefyn townsfolk had not only used the commons and wastes to graze their cattle and sheep, but it had also been their only source for cutting turfs to burn as fuel on their cottage fires. At this time there was a heavy tax on coal arriving by sea, and it was only the wealthier folk who could afford to burn coal. Moreover, many people who had built dwellings upon encroachments were to lose their homes entirely with only meagre financial compensation. Therefore it was the poorest members of the community who were to suffer most as a result of Parliamentary enclosure, which rendered their former commons and wastes 'out of bounds' to them.

In September 1812, as the clerk to the Commissioners tried to administer the Act in Nefyn, Pistyll and Llithfaen, a riotous mob of angry villagers and townsfolk pelted him with stones and clods of earth. When the army was summoned, several people were arrested, including two women. Two of the ringleaders were tried for their part in the riot and sentenced to death, although their sentences were later commuted, one of them being transported to Australia. One of the consequences of the hardship caused by enclosure was that the Nefyn parish poor rate was greatly increased, but more will be said of that in a later section.

By the middle of the 19th century, agriculture remained one of the main sources of employment for Nefyn men. Out of a total adult male population of 474 recorded on the 1851 Census Return 156 (almost one third) were detailed as 'farmers', 'agricultural labourers' or 'farm servants'. Today agriculture is still very important within the Nefyn area, and the prestigious annual Llŷn and District agricultural show, or the 'Nefyn Show' as it is called locally, is still held at Nefyn, as it has been for well over 100 years. However, the advent of mechanisation and modern farming methods has meant that very few people are now employed as agricultural workers. There is some arable farming (cereals, potatoes, carrots) and some production of beef cattle, but the emphasis now is upon sheep rearing. Sheep can be seen everywhere round Nefyn – grazing in the fields, on the upland areas and even in St Mary's churchyard!

(1) Pennant, T. *A Tour in Wales 1773-6*

(2) Jones, E.G. *A Survey of the Ancient and Present State of the County of Caernarvon by William Williams of Llandygai – Cantref Lleyn* TCHS Vol. 39 (1978)

(3) Hyde-Hall, E. *A Description of Caernarvonshire, 1809-11*

(4) Hyde-Hall, E. ibid.

(5) Pennant, T. ibid.

(6) Report on the Borough of Nefyn, 1836.

8. THE PORTS OF NEFYN AND PORTH DINLLAEN AND THE COASTAL TRADE

For hundreds of years the sea had been the means by which the people of Nefyn, Porth Dinllaen and other Llŷn coastal settlements had maintained contact with the 'outside' world, and because their gently shelving, well-protected sandy bays were ideal places from which boats could work, they developed as fishing and trading ports. After Edward I had conquered Gwynedd in the 13th century and again at the time of Elizabeth I, Nefyn was listed as one of the county's chief ports along with Conwy, Caernarfon and Pwllheli, although in respect of Caernarfon, Pwllheli and Nefyn, 'they possessed no barques, ships and vessels' of their own (*The Welsh Port Books 1550-1603*). Therefore ports like Nefyn were dependent upon the sea trade brought by visiting vessels. It should be noted that, at this time, the harbours at Nefyn and Porth Dinllaen were classified and recorded as one port.

During the 17th century, local men began to sail their own small vessels to other ports and this coastal trade seems to have been predominantly with the ports of Lancashire and Cheshire, particularly Liverpool and Chester. Herrings were an important export and a great deal of salt for curing the herrings was imported from Chester. The bard Huw Pennant referred to the large number of vessels trading between Nefyn and Chester, and Porth Dinllaen vessels like the *Matthew* and the *Mary* (1620) and the *Thomas and Jane* (1685) carried barrels of white and red herrings to Chester. The poet Morys Dwyfach, recorded that the millstone for Edern Mill was transported from Anglesey to Nefyn. In 1623 the Porth Dinllaen ship *Speedwell* sailed from Chester to Porth Dinllaen with a load of copperas, hops, pepper, logwood, cloth and a package of clay pipes. Apart from salt and the above commodities, goods imported into Nefyn at this time included iron and ironmongery items, candles, vinegar, sugar, soap, and cart wheels – 3 pairs came to Nefyn by ship in 1629.

The Port Books for Bangor 1729-30 provide details of 9 vessels belonging to the port of Nefyn with an average tonnage of 14 tons. Gradually more and more owners and captains began to set their sights upon trading with ports further afield, sailing to places like Dublin, Belfast, Cork and Waterford in Ireland; Bristol, Gloucester and Chepstow on the Severn; Whitehaven, Workington and Carlisle in the north west; Exeter, Bridport, Newhaven and Shoreham along the southern coast of

In times past the two bays at Nefyn and Porth Dinllaen, with their sheltered, gently shelving beaches, provided a safe haven for the many small coasting vessels bringing coal and shop goods to Llŷn and exporting herrings and agricultural produce.

Until the early 20th century Porth Dinllaen was a busy little port, exporting Llŷn produce and importing goods for distribution across the peninsula.

Situated on the landward side of the town is Garn Boduan on top of which may be found the remains of an Iron Age settlement.

These low lying fields are thought to have been the site of Edward I's ostentatious tournament in the summer of 1284.

Mursefer and Tŷ Receiver are a pair of 18th century semi-detached cottages built by the Nanhoron estate on the site of an earlier dwelling once owned by Humphrey Jones, Charles I's Receiver General of Revenues for North Wales.

The Nanhoron Arms Hotel was named after the Nanhoron family, who were one of the principal land owners in Nefyn.

This plaque on the wall of Bethania Chapel, Pistyll, commemorates the life and work of Tom Nefyn, the local evangelist and preacher.

Tŷ Newborough, formerly a public house called the Newborough Arms, was named after Lord Newborough of Boduan and Glynllifon, an important landowner in Nefyn.

Now called 'The Three Herrings', this building was the original Nanhoron Arms Hotel which accommodated visitors to the town during the late 19th century.

Y Ffynnon. In 1868 this stone-built structure was erected over the town's well which had provided the town with water for centuries.

Tŵr. This stone tower, built on the medieval castle motte in 1846, served as a lookout in connection with the herring fishing.

The old Customs House at Bwlch, Morfa Nefyn, was formerly used as a store for confiscated smuggled goods.

Clwb Mawr. This building in the Maes was built as an insurance office for Clwb Mawr, a Nefyn friendly society, and it was also used as a school, a place of worship for the Particular Baptists and a navigation school for training sailors.

This house, Tan y Dderwen, was one of the Nefyn ship insurance offices during the second half of the 19th century.

The scarred contours of Gwylwyr Mountain provide evidence of the Gwylwyr Quarry, the most important of the granite quarries in the Nefyn area.

The remains of the granite quarry workings at Foel Dywyrch on the Mynydd.

Capel Seion was built in 1904 to replace the smaller Baptist chapel on the Fron, where the old Baptist graveyard can still be seen.

Capel Moreia is the Wesleyan chapel built in 1881 to accommodate the growing Wesleyan congregation.

Capel Salem, Morfa Nefyn was built as a place of worship for the Congregationalists in the village.

St David's Church. The new Nefyn parish church of St David was built in 1904.

Capel Soar. This Independent chapel was erected as a replacement for the original building following the influx of Independent quarry workers from Penmaenmawr and Leicestershire.

This Life Saving Apparatus Station, situated near the children's playground in Morfa, was built in 1864 to house a horse-drawn wagon containing items of shore to ship rescue equipment.

Ysgol Nefyn. This building facing the road is the original undenominational British School built by public subscription in 1859. Later, following the 1870 Education Act, it housed the Nefyn Board School.

Whitehall, Porth Dinllaen. When plans were drawn up for Porth Dinllaen to become the seaport and packet station for Ireland in the early 19th century this building with its archway was designed to be a hotel.

The sailing ship weather vane on the tower of the old St Mary's Church now serves as a reminder of Nefyn's ancient maritime tradition.

The Tŷ Coch Inn, Porth Dinllaen served the needs of local sailors and shipbuilders for decades, and it was here that Mrs Jane Jones, the only female harbourmaster in Britain, lived and also ran a school.

A view of Nefyn from Gwylwyr Mynydd with the two bays of Porth Nefyn and Porth Dinllaen beyond.

Stryd y Ffynnon, Nefyn, dated 1905.

44

Cliff walk, Nefyn.

Fishermen with their boats at Nefyn and a sloop at anchor, dated 1907.

45

The Castle and the cliff top path, Nefyn, in the early 1950's.

Porth Nefyn and the beach road in the mid 20th century.

Stooks of corn drying in a field overlooking the bay at Morfa Nefyn.

Portdinllaen, with Nevin Point and The Rivals.

The cluster of buildings at Bwlch, including the old Customs House, 1905.

The beach at Bwlch in 1905, showing the wooden jetty and the chimney stack belonging to the brickworks.

Morfa Nefyn from above, looking across the bay towards Yr Eifl, circa 1970.

England; London, Ipswich, King's Lynn, Hull and Newcastle on the east coast; and Dumfries, Glasgow, Greenock and Leith in Scotland

Coastwise traffic increased greatly during the late 18th and early 19th centuries. In 1804 655 vessels are on record as having entered Porth Dinllaen and Porth Nefyn. By 1840 914 ships were putting into the bays and in 1861 over 700 vessels are recorded as still visiting. However, it is probable that many of those vessels arrived at Porth Dinllaen rather than Nefyn, for there is still no distinction in the records between the two ports. Moreover, it must be recognised that some ships on passage to other destinations may simply have been seeking shelter in the bay during stormy weather rather than putting into port.

The main export from Nefyn during the 18th and early 19th centuries continued to be salted and bloatered herrings. In 1747 Lewis Morris recorded that nearly 5000 barrels of salted herrings were sent from Nefyn during that year. A Nefyn merchant, Charles Prichard, sent barrels of herrings to Dublin in a small sloop of 20 tons captained by John Howell. At about the same time Robert Rowland took another 30 barrels to the same port in the *Speedwell*.

In addition to herrings, large quantities of cereals and farm produce were exported through Nefyn and Porth Dinllaen, and 4 out of every 5 cargoes went to Liverpool. Pennant (1773-6) stated that "much oats, barley, butter and cheese are exported"[1] from Llŷn. Writing of Nefyn in 1809-11, Edmund Hyde-Hall referred to the "coasters which supply the Liverpool market from this neighbourhood with poultry, shell fish and other small articles"[2]. Samuel Lewis (1834) emphasised the trade with Liverpool in eggs, poultry and pigs, while the Report on the Borough of Nefyn (1836) mentioned that Nefyn exported corn, butter and cheese. Throughout the 19th century large numbers of pigs were exported from the area through Porth Dinllaen, for pigs were one of the chief agricultural products of the Nefyn district for many years. From the 1830's and 1840's they were carried to Liverpool in steamships like the *Vale of Clwyd*, the *Snowdon* and the *Monk*. But cargoes of pigs were also transported in sailing vessels, such as the Nefyn sloop *Sea Lark* in 1833 and the brig *Antelope* in 1840.

During the early 18th century slate began to be exported from North Wales to ports like Chester, Liverpool, Flint and Milford Haven as well as places further afield, and some of it was carried in Nefyn vessels like the *Speedwell*. In 1730 one load of 6000 slates was taken from Caernarfon to Porth Dinllaen. During the late 18th century and early 19th century Nefyn ships and seamen (like the *Brunswick* captained by Hugh Ellis of Mursefer, Nefyn) carried Ffestiniog slates from Ynys Cyngar in the

Glaslyn Estuary. Subsequently Nefyn-owned and manned ships carried Ffestiniog slates from the wharves at Porthmadog; they transported Nantlle slates from Caernarfon, Llanberis slates from Y Felinheli and Penrhyn slates from Port Penrhyn, Bangor. According to one source, in 1813 Nefyn provided about 30 ships carrying slates from Caernarfon.

Another significant Caernarfonshire industry in the 18th century was the burning of seaweed and bracken to produce seaweed ashes and bracken ashes for export to the soap-making workshops of Liverpool, Warrington, Chester and Bristol. This trade continued until about the middle of the 19th century, and a peck of ashes would sell for 6 shillings. At Porth Dinllaen harbour in 1806 the port duty was set at 18 pence per ton for bracken ashes and 1 shilling per ton for seaweed ashes.

Cargoes imported into Nefyn and Porth Dinllaen in the 18th and 19th centuries included salt, wood, limestone, shop and soap waste, culm, coal and miscellaneous shop goods. In 1736 a vessel carrying salt from Cheshire began to leak during a storm in 'Ridland Bay' and the cargo had to be thrown overboard. In 1759 the sloop *Speedwell* of Nefyn sprang a leak whilst carrying a cargo of salt, which was badly damaged as a result of water penetration into the hold. Salt houses were built along the bay at Nefyn and at Wern, while others were situated in the town at Tan y Maes ('Ty Halen') and on the shore at Bwlch, Morfa Nefyn. The tax on salt was very heavy (30 shillings a ton during the Napoleonic Wars) and this resulted in much salt smuggling.

Wood was imported into Nefyn and Porth Dinllaen, mainly to service the shipbuilding industry. Oak came from Conwy – 3 loads to Nefyn and 1 to Porth Dinllaen during 1854-5. Baltic and Canadian pine was also imported for the shipbuilding and for house building. Limestone was shipped inwards via these Llŷn ports for burning in local limekilns in Porth Nefyn and at Porth Dinllaen. The lime was used to make both lime mortar for house building and fertilizer to be spread on the fields. Soap and shop waste (soap sediment and the waste from shops) was frequently the preferred ballast on ships travelling back from Dublin, for it was considered to be a very powerful manure for the land, thus commanding a good price.

From the 18th century to the early 20th century increasing amounts of culm and coal were imported into Nefyn and Porth Dinllaen by sea. At first coal could be afforded only by the wealthy gentry and yeoman farmers owing to its cost, but by the second half of the 19th century, after the tax on sea borne coal had been abolished, coal fires burned in many of the cottage grates in Nefyn. Coal was transported in sailing ships from places like Liverpool, Chester, Flint, Mostyn, Neath, Swansea and

Newcastle. The coal ships would run onto the sandy beach at high tide, and when the sea had gone out teams of horses and carts would carry the fuel away to local coal yards. There were 3 coal yards in Nefyn; one at Tan y Maes, one in Stryd Fawr and one at the bottom of Stryd y Ffynnon where the Fire Station now stands. There were other coal yards in Porth Dinllaen where, in later years, an offshore wooden platform was constructed at Bwlch so that vessels could berth in the water to be unloaded by means of buckets travelling from ship to shore on an aerial system of wires and pulleys. In the period between the two World Wars, steamers such as the *Tryfan* and the *Maggie Purvis* regularly brought shipments of coal to Porth Dinllaen until the outbreak of the Second World War.

Coasting vessels were the means by which the towns and villages of Llŷn were supplied with a variety of shop goods from Liverpool, ranging from groceries and textiles to medical and building supplies. At first such goods were carried in sailing sloops and small schooners. Later, until the outbreak of the First World War, steamships of the Aberdovey and Barmouth Steamship Company (first the *Telephone* and afterwards the *Dora*) regularly called at Porth Dinllaen, where consignments of 'inwards' goods were stored in a warehouse on the beach, known locally as 'Warws Dora', before being distributed to shops throughout the district. This warehouse, a corrugated iron structure built up on pillars, can still be seen as you walk across the beach towards the cluster of buildings at the far end of Porth Dinllaen.

Coasting vessels were also the means by which many Llŷn folk maintained contact with friends and relatives in other parts. It was not unusual for inhabitants of Nefyn to travel to Caernarfon by sea for a meeting or to visit relatives, either occupying a place upon the open deck amidst the cargo or, for an increased charge, enjoying a place within the relative comfort of the cabin. A small package or a written message was sometimes carried from Nefyn to Liverpool by an obliging ship's captain, so that it could be delivered to a member of the large expatriate Welsh community living in that port. As Directories record, from the 1840's steam packets like the *Dolphin* and the *Skimmer* ran a regular weekly service from Porth Dinllaen to Liverpool, while an advertisement in the North Wales Chronicle for 1839 records that the steamer *Eclipse* ran a regular weekly service from Liverpool, carrying goods and passengers, calling at Bangor, Caernarfon, Porth Dinllaen and Barmouth.

Although there were stone-built piers at both Nefyn and Porth Dinllaen as early as 1747 when Lewis Morris drew up his chart of *'Porthdinlleyn and Nevyn Bay and Harbour'*, neither bay developed into a substantial port like Porthmadog, Caernarfon or Pwllheli. Lewis Morris stated that the Porth Dinllaen pier erected during the reign of George I was never completed and would soon be in ruins if not looked after. Nefyn sailors and fishermen petitioned for the Nefyn pier to be reconstructed in 1808 and again in 1830, while several fruitless requests were made to Squire Madryn, the principal owner of Porth Dinllaen harbour, for improvements to be made to the pier and harbour there.

Both ports continued to receive some ships throughout the 19th century and into the 20th century. The 1836 Nefyn Report recorded that, on average, 36 vessels came to Porth Nefyn each year to discharge coal and shop goods and to export agricultural produce. Ships continued to bring coal and to carry away setts from the Gwylwyr Quarry until the outbreak of the First World War. But Porth Dinllaen had assumed the role of chief port along the northern coast of Llŷn. In 1863 196 vessels came to Porth Dinllaen carrying goods inwards and 28 ships went out with cargoes. As late as 1880 128 vessels took goods inwards and 84 carried cargoes outwards. Porth Dinllaen was able to boast a harbour master (Mrs. Jane Jones of Tŷ Coch, the only female harbour master in Britain) until the 1920's. During the first half of the 19th century, Porth Dinllaen had been considered one of the best pier harbours in Wales and, as will be seen in a later section, vain attempts were made to turn it into the packet station for Ireland instead of Holyhead.

Well before the 1880's coastal seaborne traffic was in decline, for the railways were offering a faster and more convenient means of transport to the larger centres of population. Although some Nefyn sailors continued to engage in coastal sailing, by this time more and more shipowners and captains were turning their attention to alternative and more profitable trading routes to distant and exotic destinations across the oceans.

(1) Pennant, T. *A Tour in Wales, 1773-6*
(2) Hyde-Hall, E. *A Description of Caernarvonshire 1809-11*

9. CUSTOMS DUTIES AND SMUGGLING AROUND NEFYN

For centuries taxes have been levied on a variety of goods coming into Britain. Such duties have tended to be at their highest during wartime when governments needed increased revenue to pay for the hostilities. Historically, commodities which have been taxed have included every day items like salt, coal, soap, sugar and tea as well as luxuries such as silk, tobacco, wines and spirits.

Just as governments have always sought to raise revenue by imposing customs duties on goods coming into the country, so there have always been people determined to avoid payment of those taxes. Of course, the remote Llŷn coastline, with its many rocky creeks and sandy bays, was an ideal place to land and dispose of illicit goods. There is evidence of smuggling and piracy in the seas around Llŷn during Elizabethan times, but smuggling was at its height in these parts during the 17th and 18th centuries. Porth Dinllaen was the centre of smuggling activity along the northern coast of Llŷn, and local inhabitants, including members of the gentry and clergy, saw nothing dishonest in trading with and even assisting the smugglers. Farmers and cottagers helped to unload the contraband and 'spirit' it away rapidly using horses and carts and donkeys. In his report of 1763 the captain of the local Revenue cutter stated that the smugglers never attempted to land their illicit goods before midnight and within an hour of their doing so, the entire cargo had been unloaded and hidden away.

The prevention of smuggling was in the hands of Revenue Officers; one team, based in Nefyn covered the northern coast of Llŷn and the other at Pwllheli was responsible for the southern coast. In the 1780's there were 5 Revenue men resident in Nefyn – Mr. Robert Lloyd, Pen y Graig (Salt and Customs Officer), John Ellis, Tŷ Cerrig and William Hughes, Fron Deg (both Salt Officers), John Williams, Cae Rhug (Customs Officer) and Mr. Edward Banton, Pen y Maes (Excise Officer). There are a great many references in the Nefyn Parish Registers and the Nefyn Court Book to 'Officers', the earliest being Roberts Lloyd, Salt Officer, who was buried on the 28th January, 1744.

The precise extent of smuggling is very difficult to establish because, by its very nature, it was a secretive activity and therefore evidence is fragmentary. In the late 17th century two smuggling vessels carrying brandy put into various places along the northern coast of Llŷn including Porth Dinllaen, but it is said that they were not able to sell much of their

53

contraband because the local inhabitants were already well supplied. There is a record of a smuggling ship which went ashore at Porth Dinllaen in 1783, both vessel and crew being captured. A famous local smuggler of the early 19th century was Boaz Prichard, a Caernarfon merchant and shopkeeper. In his sloop, *Lively*, it is said he frequently smuggled brandy from the Channel Islands to Porth Dinllaen and other places in Llŷn. He was finally caught in 1838 with 99 casks of illegal brandy at his house in Caernarfon and was committed to Caernarfon gaol. The name 'Brandy Boaz' has become a part of Llŷn folklore.

Sometimes well-armed smugglers were prepared to use violence to avoid capture and on occasions there were open clashes between the local inhabitants and the forces of law and order. In 1673 smugglers were discovered unloading a cargo at Porth Dinllaen but the authorities were unable to intervene because the smugglers were too well armed. In 1773 an armed smuggling vessel the *Fox* was sighted off the Llŷn coast by the Revenue cutter *Hector* but the vessel escaped. There was a report of a serious riot in Nefyn in 1726.

Frequently smugglers used more devious methods of avoiding detection, but not always with success. In 1734 Thomas Owen of Tŷ Mawr, Nefyn, had his vessel the *Royal George* confiscated because, having taken a consignment of lobsters and crabs to Liverpool, he returned with a cargo of hemp, flax and cloth for a Nefyn shopkeeper. But Officers also found nearly a ton of coal hidden on board, which he claimed was loaded in error when he requested some ballast for the return journey. When a smuggling vessel arrived at Porth Dinllaen in 1791, the Revenue Officers boarding her were taken by surprise and locked in a cabin until all the goods had been unloaded, only to be released as the ship set sail again. In 1774 Officers found a barrel of brandy hidden in a hedge near the house of Richard Jones, labourer, of Nefyn. On the beach at Bwlch, Morfa Nefyn is a tall house called Tŷ Newydd, which was once used as a customs house. Here, confiscated contraband was stored on the upper floor, and it is reported that thieves, determined to steal the spirits from the barrels deposited upstairs, would gain entry to the ground floor and drill up through the floor boards into the bottom of the casks above, gathering the liquid into cans as it tricked down below. It is said that, until several years ago, the plugged holes could still be seen in those floorboards.

The two taxes which affected the people of Nefyn most were the duties on salt and coal. The salt tax was an ancient one, revived by Walpole in the first half of the 18th century, but during the Napoleonic Wars it became a crippling burden for the fishermen of Nefyn. As huge quantities of salt were required for processing the fish, it is little wonder that there was much salt theft and smuggling. In 1786 John Robert, a Nefyn mariner was summoned to appear before the Quarter Sessions, having been accused by Richard Coytmore, Salt Officer, of taking and carrying away a quantity of salt. In the same year two more Nefyn mariners were fined at the Quarter Sessions for stealing salt.

The duty on coal dated back to the reign of William III and was raised only on coal which was transported by sea. For a long time this had been a bone of contention among the Caernarfonshire gentry and the more affluent yeoman farmers, who depended upon sea- borne coal because its transport over land was almost impossible owing to the poor state of the roads. When the large scale enclosures of the early 19th century deprived small farmers and cottagers of the right to cut turfs for fuel from the wastes, the coal tax began to impose a very heavy burden upon the mass of the ordinary folk. The coal regulations and duty also caused much aggravation for the ships' captains transporting it, since the customs officer at Porth Dinllaen had to measure each cargo of coal before the vessel could leave. In 1815 with many coal ships waiting to be unloaded, there developed a heated dispute between the ships' captains and David Wilson, the Porth Dinllaen customs officer, who was prevented from going from ship to ship with his measuring tub. W.A. Madocks (MP for Boston in Lincolnshire, who owned an estate at Penmorfa) battled hard in Parliament for the abolition of the tax on sea-borne coal, which was eventually lifted. The disappearance of the duties on salt and coal in the 1820's and early 1830's brought about a great reduction in the amount of smuggling. The author of the 1836 Report on the Borough of Nefyn wrote, "There is no smuggling here now. I do not remember any except of salt." However, as late as 1851, there were still 2 customs officers resident within the parish.

10. SHIPBUILDING AND SHIP REPAIRING AT PORTH NEFYN

As the men of Nefyn had established a tradition of building their own fishing boats on the beach of Nefyn, it is not surprising that, sooner or later, they should have used their skills to start building and repairing larger vessels. The ships known to have been built here over a period of 150 years included sloops, smacks, snows, schooners, brigs, brigantines and barques. These classifications all refer to the rig of the vessel. Sloops and schooners are rigged fore and aft with triangular shaped sails. A sloop is a small one-masted boat rigged fore and aft with a mainsail and a jib, while a schooner has 2 or more masts rigged fore and aft. Snows, brigs, brigantines and barques are all partly or predominantly square rigged vessels. A snow has 2 masts each with square sails; a brig is a two-masted square-rigged ship with an additional lower fore and aft sail; a brigantine also has 2 masts, the foremast square-rigged and the mainmast rigged fore and aft; a barque is a three-masted vessel with the rear mast rigged fore and aft and the remaining masts square-rigged.

There is no documentary evidence about the building of most of the early vessels constructed in North Wales. The first vessel recorded as 'built at Nefyn' was the *Hopewell*, a 17 ton sloop built in 1760. Its details are written down in the Beaumaris Shipping Registers, which were commenced in 1786. These registers record the details of a number of vessels built prior to 1786, but they include only those vessels built pre-1786 which were re-registered after that date. Therefore details are not available for the majority of vessels built before 1786. Two other ships built at Nefyn in the 1760's and re-registered post-1786 are the 15 ton sloop *Mary* built in 1767 and the 30 ton sloop *Peggy* built in 1768.

The increase in coastal trading, the growth of the port of Liverpool and the development of the North Wales slate trade all gave impetus to the need for local wooden sailing ships. Between 1770 and 1830 46 vessels with a total tonnage of 2,183 tons are known to have been built on Nefyn beach, and during this period Nefyn was the fourth most important shipbuilding centre in Caernarfonshire after Pwllheli, Caernarfon and Conwy. Between 1830 and 1880 a further 86 vessels were built at Porth Nefyn with an aggregate tonnage of 7,977 tons and, during these years within the county, only Porthmadog and Pwllheli built more ships and a greater tonnage of shipping.

During the 18th century the vessels built at Nefyn were mainly sloops of between 14 and 30 tons, with the exception of the *Prince of Orange* (a 78 ton brigantine built in 1784) and the *Peggy* (a 50 ton sloop built in 1788). By the 1830's, fewer sloops were being built and more schooners, brigs and brigantines of under 100 tons were being launched from Nefyn beach. One or two vessels were over 100 tons, such as the brigantine *Waterloo* (built 1815 -104 tons), the brig *Antelope* (built 1828 – 106 tons), the schooner *Cevn Amwlch* (built 1838 – 110 tons) and 3 schooners built in 1839 the *Superior* (121 tons), the *Jane and Ellen* (111 tons) and the *Vron* (101 tons).

By 1850, the advent of the railways and the availability of cheaper wooden vessels from North America (mainly Quebec, Prince Edward Island, New Brunswick and Nova Scotia) had slowed down the North Wales shipbuilding industry. Fewer ships were now being built at Nefyn during the second half of the 19th century, but they tended to be better designed and more skilfully built. By this time, Nefyn-built vessels were mainly the larger vessels of well over 100 tons such as the barque *Robert Thomas* (1855 – 335 tons), the brigantine Nanhoron (1859 – 147 tons), the barque *Isolina* (1866 – 390 tons) and the 3 masted schooner *Ebenezer Parry* (1877 – 193 tons). The last ship to leave the stocks at Porth Nefyn was the 107 ton schooner *Venus* which was completed in 1880.

By the 1880's local shipbuilding in North Wales had virtually ceased. Only the Porthmadog yards survived to build the distinctive ocean-going wooden schooners called Western Ocean Yachts up until the outbreak of the First World War. There were several reasons for the demise of the North Wales shipbuilding industry - the depression in the local slate industry, the coming of the railways and the preference for steamers all helped to depress the coastal trade and to put an end to the demand for wooden-built coasting vessels. Furthermore, the invention of the superior triple expansion steam engine and the preference for larger ships built of iron and steel, which had become much cheaper to build, virtually signed the death warrant of the ocean-going wooden barque, brigantine and three-masted schooner.

Who were these men who built ships in places like Nefyn? Originally they were mariners, farmers and fishermen who saw the need for small sloops and smacks to carry local produce to the centres of population such as Liverpool and Dublin. David Thomas has identified over 20 shipbuilders who built vessels on Nefyn beach, but the names of those who built vessels prior to about 1810 will probably never be known. Among the more notable 19th century shipbuilders are William Roberts, Penpalment, who built at least 7 vessels from 1833-48; Hugh Roberts, Groes, who built at least 6 vessels from 1837-45; Richard Davies, Stryd y Ffynnon, who built 8 ships from 1839-49; Owen Griffith, Plas, who is known to have built 4 ships between 1856-62; and Griffith Owen, Dyffryn, who built 5 ships from 1872-1880, all of which sailed for over 20 years, two of them lasting for more than 40 years.

The most famous of the early 19th century Nefyn shipbuilders was John John Thomas of Vron Oleu. He was a fisherman, merchant, shipowner, shipbuilder and farmer, and he was known locally as 'Brenin Nefyn' (King Nefyn). At first, it is said, he employed many men in the herring fishing, building his own small fishing boats. Indeed, he sold salted herrings mainly to Irish ships which called at Nefyn. Then he started to build his own ships to export his herrings, and the natural progression from this was to build ships for other local folk. He employed carpenters and joiners to carry out this work, and from 1813 to 1839 he built at least 15 vessels, including the sloop *Arvonia* (1813 – 70 tons), the sloop *Talysarn* (68 tons), the brig *Zebra* (1825 – 91 tons), the brig *Ardent* (1826 – 93 tons), the schooner *Madryn* (1836 – 81 tons) and the schooner *Vron* (1839 – 101 tons). His reputation in Nefyn is legendary, for it is said that every week he used to walk to the bank in Caernarfon to obtain the money to pay his workforce. He had to walk the lonely path over Yr Eifl and apparently he was never attacked and robbed, for it is said that he was a formidably strong man.

Robert Thomas, Y Dderwen, allegedly employing a workforce of 100 men, built 13 ships at Nefyn between 1849 and 1866. His vessels included the schooner *Sedulous* (1849 – 74 tons), the barque *Robert Thomas* (1855 – 335 tons), the schooner *Polly Preston* (1863 – 131 tons), the brigantine *Nanhoron* (1859 – 147 tons) and the barque *Isolina* (1866 – 390 tons). Wooden ships of the very highest quality usually lasted for between 10 and 20 years. Of Robert Thomas's ships 8 sailed for more than 20 years, of which 3 sailed for 32-34 years, and 2 lasted for 40 years.

A considerable amount of work for Nefyn shipbuilders also came from repairing and altering ships. Some vessels were enlarged by sawing them in half and inserting a complete new middle section, thus increasing the length, the tonnage and often altering the rig. For example, the *Mary Watkins* built at Nefyn in 1850 was later lengthened from 73ft to 92 ft. and her tonnage was increased from 130 tons to 169 tons.

Many occupations were involved in the shipbuilding. According to the 1851 Census there were 42 men living within the parish of Nefyn who may have been directly involved in shipbuilding. There were 8 'shipbuilders', 2 'shipwrights', 30 'carpenters' or 'ship's carpenters', 2 'sawyers', 5 'blacksmiths', 3 'nailers', 1 'painter', 1 'turner' and 1 'brazier'. No sail makers, block makers and rope makers were mentioned, although in the case of 13 men no occupation was given. But not all the men working in the Nefyn shipbuilding were men from the parish. Each morning workmen walked to Porth Nefyn from surrounding inland and coastal villages. Many of the local public footpaths which exist today are the same paths which ship workers and mariners trod 150 years ago. During the 19th century, there were 2 Nefyn saw pits for sawing timber - one at Cefn y Maes and another in the Stryd Fawr. Sails were produced in the sail lofts in Stryd fawr and Marine Terrace. There were 3 ropewalks producing ropes – one at Tan y Maes, one at Marine Terrace and another at the Felin (the mill). Nefyn had 2 block makers' workshops at Tan y Maes and Cae Rhyg. Several nailer's workshops and blacksmiths' forges produced nails and ironwork such as chain plates. Others existed in Morfa and Porth Dinllaen to service the shipbuilding there.

Oak was imported from Conwy and sometimes shipbuilders, like William Roberts in 1845 and Hugh Roberts in 1846, made requests to local estate owners, like Lord Newborough, for hardwood logs if they were felling trees on their estates. Pine timbers were imported from the Baltic and from Canada. A launching was a very important event at a shipbuilding centre. Crowds would gather to watch the ceremony and to see the vessel enter the water. A minister of religion would stand on the deck to bless the vessel with a prayer, sometimes preaching a sermon to the assembled crowds. After the ceremony the shipbuilder often gave a celebratory meal for his friends and another for the workmen who had built the vessel.

Of the ships which David Thomas identified as being built at Nefyn, 72% were eventually lost at sea. However, of the Nefyn-built ships for which full details are available, 66% lasted for more than 20 years, while 25% continued to sail for more than 40 years. These statistics stand as a tribute to the skill of the men who designed and built those vessels, as well as to the fine seamanship of the sailors who sailed them.

11. NEFYN SEAMEN AND THE FOREIGN MARITIME TRADE

As the coastal trade began to decline and as the global maritime trade expanded, more and more shipowners saw that there were greater financial gains to be made from vessels which sailed far beyond the coasts of Britain to more distant trading destinations. More and more Nefyn men began to captain and man the ships which sailed the oceans of the world. These ocean-going trading vessels carried all manner of cargoes including slates, grain, phosphate, nitrate, coal, rock salt, fish, flour, cement, linseed, tea, coffee, sugar, rice, jute, wool, timber and the smelliest but perhaps one of the most profitable cargoes of all – guano.

The expansion of the North Wales slate trade gave an enormous boost to the foreign maritime trade from the ports of Caernarfonshire during the 19th century. North Wales slates were exported world wide, principally from Porthmadog and Bangor, and Nefyn-owned and managed ships, manned largely by Nefyn sea captains and sailors, played their part. Nefyn sailors manned the vessels which carried cargoes of slate to Denmark, Norway, Sweden, Holland, France and the German Baltic ports, as well as to ports in the Mediterranean, the Adriatic, the United States and South America. In 1842 a disastrous fire destroyed much of the old city of Hamburg and vast quantities of Penrhyn and Ffestiniog slates were used in the reconstruction of that city.

A popular trading route was the triangular voyage from North Wales to continental Europe, then across the Atlantic to Canada, and finally back across to the Mediterranean before returning home. Many a Nefyn seaman sailed from Porthmadog to Hamburg or Stettin with a cargo of Ffestiniog slates. From here the ship would make its way to the Spanish port of Cadiz where it was loaded up with salt, which was taken across to the fishing ports of Labrador and Newfoundland. Here the ship would take on board a cargo of dried and salted codfish bound for a Mediterranean port, where having discharged the fish cargo, it was loaded with citrus fruits and olive oil destined for Britain.

Nefyn mariners were also involved in the North African grain trade, sailing between Porthmadog and the Atlantic coastal towns of Morocco such as Casablanca, where they anchored off the beaches to take on board their loads. This was a very profitable trade but it was not without its dangers. The weather on this Atlantic coast can be very unpredictable and a commodity like grain can easily shift in the ship's hold, making the vessel very unstable.

Some Nefyn sailors manned the vessels which sailed to the tropical island of Aruba, part of the Dutch Antilles, lying off the coast of Venezuela. Here the ships were loaded up with phosphate rock, quarried in the interior of the island and brought to a makeshift quay on the coast at Fort Zoutman via a jerry-built narrow gauge railway. Transporting phosphate rock was not a pleasant task. The approach to the harbour was obstructed by dangerous coral reefs, and as the phosphate was tipped into the ship's hold, everything and everybody was covered with a horrible choking white dust. These phosphate-carrying square riggers (mainly brigs, brigantines and barquentines) were so weighed down by their heavy loads that some of them were in danger of not making it back across the Atlantic.

Nefyn men were also involved in the shipment of timber from the Baltic and from Canada. The ship 'Planet' belonging to Griffith Owen, the Nefyn shipbuilder, used to carry timber from the Baltic. Other Nefyn mariners sailed in vessels which transported sugar, molasses, coffee and spices from the Caribbean, from Brazil and from the Spanish Main ports like Para, Demerara and Paramaribo. Some carried tea from India, Ceylon and China and many a Nefyn sailor rounded the Horn into the Pacific to load up with nitrate at the Chilean ports of Topacilla, Callao and Antafagasta, or to take on board cargoes of guano from the Chincha Islands off the coast of Peru.

Before signing up a crew for a voyage, the captain would make clear the ship's anticipated destination. Normally a specific port would be detailed and then other possible destinations, regions or latitudes would be specified. For example, in June 1867, the *Rebecca* captained by Hugh Parry of Stryd y Ffynnon, Nefyn was scheduled to "sail to Hamburg and then to any other port between Brest and the Elbe"[1]. The anticipated duration of the voyage was also part of the terms and conditions of engagement. A voyage was detailed "not to exceed 3 months" or "6 months" or 12 months" and so on. Sometimes the larger barques and fully-rigged ships would be away from port for as long as 3 years, as they criss-crossed the oceans many times, carrying cargoes from continent to continent.

In February 1901 the *Gwrtheyrn Castle*, captained by Captain William Davies of Stryd y Ffynnon, Nefyn sailed from Liverpool to Brisbane (Queensland, Australia) and then south to Newcastle (New South Wales). From Newcastle she sailed across the Indian Ocean to Mauritius and then back to Sydney (New South Wales). Her next destination took her back across the Indian Ocean again to Cape Town (South Africa), then back to Sydney and up to Newcastle once more. From eastern Australia she sailed across the Pacific Ocean to Coquimbo and Pisagua (both in Chile). Next she rounded Cape Horn and sailed northwards across the Atlantic to dock in Falmouth. From Falmouth she sailed up the English Channel, across to Rotterdam and then on to Antwerp. Finally she arrived back in Liverpool in July, 1903, concluding a voyage which had lasted nearly two and a half years.

Throughout the later decades of the 19th century and the early years of the 20th century, oceanic sailing came to dominate the life of this little town, which provided so many of the captains and seamen who sailed, not only locally-owned vessels, but also sailing ships of the mercantile fleet belonging to the large British shipping companies based in ports like Liverpool and London. Seafaring had become a tradition within many Nefyn families, for it was usual for young men to follow fathers and grandfathers to sea, although the merchant navy also provided an alternative means of livelihood for the sons of farmers, fishermen and quarrymen. The sea was 'in the blood' of Nefyn folk, and as Aledd Eames has pointed out, the talk within the town was often of distant places like "Callao. 'Frisco, Valpariso, Akyab, Bombay or Melbourne"[2]. By the closing years of the 19th century the mantelpieces and window sills of many Nefyn cottages and houses were crammed with mementoes brought back from far-off and exotic locations, for these were the places that husbands, fathers and sons visited during the course of their work.

(1) Crew Lists and Agreements for 'Rebecca' No. 363765.
(2) Eames, A. *Ventures in Sail*

12. SHIP OWNERSHIP

Throughout the years of sail the local system of ship ownership in Nefyn, and indeed in other Welsh ports, was a co-operative one. The ownership of each vessel was divided into 64ths, and a number of different shareholders would each purchase shares in a particular vessel, which was captained by someone in whom they had confidence. This local shareholding was vitally important to the entire maritime economy. In the early days such investments made by local people provided the capital to finance the vessels which exported goods away from the area and which brought in the wide range of commodities required for everyday living.

During the 18th century it was quite common for a small sloop to be owned by 2 or 3 individuals. For example, on 30th September 1786 the 27 ton sloop *Jenny*, built at Aberystwyth in 1771, was owned jointly by John Prichard and Dikus Parry, both Nefyn mariners. As vessels became larger and more costly, it was more usual for there to be several joint owners, sometimes as many as a dozen or more.

There were two kinds of shareholders – subscribing owners who signed the shipping register (often the majority shareholders, sometimes including the ship's master) and non-subscribing owners. For the most part, those owning shares in vessels were the local middle classes, which included shipbuilders (who often retained a financial interest in the vessels they built), master mariners, merchants, carriers, shopkeepers, craftsmen, farmers, innkeepers, doctors, ministers of religion, widows (of any of the above), and spinsters (frequently the sisters of ships' captains or the daughters of other shareholders). It is interesting to note that there is little evidence of the local landowning gentry investing in shipping shares.

If the subscribing owners came from Nefyn, the majority of the other shareholders also tended to be Nefyn folk, the remainder coming mainly from other surrounding Llŷn parishes. Occasionally a shareholder resided in a distant port such as Liverpool or Bristol, and often such men were sail makers, rope makers, anchor makers, merchants or ships' chandlers. There was often a strong family link between the shareholders of a Nefyn ship, for relatives and friends of the master frequently invested in the vessel which he sailed.

Family connections in local ship ownership are well illustrated by the following example:-

The Arvonia of Pwllheli, a sloop of 73 tons built at Nefyn in 1813. Master – John Ellis, Y Maes, Nefyn.[1]

| Subscribing | John Ellis | Nefyn | Mariner | 12 |

Owners	William Davies	Llanerchymedd, Anglesey	Rope-maker	4
Non-subscribing	Evan Jones	Nefyn	Merchant	8
Owners	Charles Jones	Nefyn	Mariner	2
	John Jones	Nefyn	Mariner	2
	Robert Hughes	Nefyn	Mariner	4
	Hugh Charles	Nefyn	Mariner	4
	William Ellis	Nefyn	Shopkeeper	8
	Elizabeth Ellis	Nefyn	Widow of Hugh Ellis mariner	4
	Griffith William	Pistyll	Farmer	4
	William Owen	Boduan	Mariner	4
	Jane Jones	Bryncroes	Widow of William Jones farmer	4
	William Parr	Liverpool	Book-keeper	4
	Total shares			64

Elizabeth Ellis was the widowed mother of John Ellis, the master. Evan Jones was John Ellis's father-in-law and Charles Jones and John Jones were the sons of Evan Jones and therefore John Ellis's brothers-in-law. Jane Jones was probably Evan Jones's sister-in-law, while William Ellis may have been a relative, perhaps the uncle of John Ellis. Robert Hughes was certainly closely associated with the Ellis family because his name appears on the will of Hugh Ellis (John's brother).

There was considerable buying and selling of shares in a maritime community and some people held shares in several different vessels. John Ellis held shares not only in his own vessel, *Arvonia*, but also in *Margaretta, Lady Newborough, Rhydland Leader, Gleaner, Express, Lord William Paget, Britannia, Gratitude, Ardent, Dove* and *Ann and Laura*. Over a number of years captains tended to build up their shareholding in the vessel of which they were the master. In January 1825 John Ellis held 12 shares in *Arvonia*. By the time of his death in 1848 he owned sixty 64ths of this vessel.

By the middle of the 19th century some ships were owned outright by one individual owner, often the ship's master. In 1851 the 84 ton brig *Gleaner* built at Nefyn in 1820 was owned entirely by Owen Jones, mariner, of Nefyn. It was the ambition of many a young sea captain to increase his shareholding in a small vessel until eventually he became the sole owner of that ship. Subsequently his aim was to accumulate sufficient capital to purchase a newer larger vessel. This is well illustrated by the career of Ebenezer Parry of Fron and later Stryd y Ffynnon, Nefyn.

In 1831 27 year old Ebenezer became master of the 47 ton sloop *Eleanor*

Shipbuilding on the beach at Porth Nefyn, circa 1880.

Coach and horses outside the old Nanhoron Arms, now called The Three Herrings.

Gwylwyr Quarry with wooden jetty for loading ships, dated 1906.

Sloops at anchor in the bay at Nefyn, dated 1907.

Stryd y Ffynnon, circa 1910.

Bwlch with evidence of the ship-to-shore apparatus for unloading coal ships moored offshore, circa 1910.

Sailing vessel unloading goods at Warws Dora, Porth Dinllaen, circa 1910.

Church choral festival procession to St David's Church, dated 1912.

Stryd Fawr, Nefyn. Note the early lorry to the right and on the opposite side of the road the charabanc advertising Sunday tours.

The bay at Abergeirch, the terminus of the telegraph cable from Ireland, dated 1917.

Holiday-makers relaxing on the beach, dated 1919.

The town of Nefyn photographed from the Mynydd, dated 1922.

View across the fields towards Carreg Lefain and Gwylwyr, dated 1925.

The beach road and the bay at Nefyn, dated 1930.

71

1930's view of the bay at Nefyn with Bodeilias, Carreg y Llam, Yr Eifl and the Gwylwyr Quarry jetty.

Porth Nefyn in the 1930's.

The old turnpike road through Boduan woods to Pwllheli.

The road from Nefyn to Morfa Nefyn.

The café half way down the road to the beach at Nefyn, dated 1949.

The beach and cliffs at Nefyn, dated 1951.

Visitors sitting on the rocks at Porth Nefyn, dated 1952.

Vehicles parked above the beach at Nefyn, early 1950's.

The café on the road to the beach at Nefyn, early 1950's.

The cottages at Porth Nefyn, early 1950's.

The old St Mary's Church and churchyard at Penisa'r dre, Nefyn.

Pony rides on Nefyn beach.

The cluster of cottages nestling beneath the cliffs of Penrhyn Nefyn.

Holiday-makers on the beach at Morfa Nefyn.

78

The lifeboat station and slipway at Porth Dinllaen.

Looking across the bay from Porth Dinllaen towards Yr Eifl.

Porth Nefyn 1960s.

and Jane. He took over the captaincy from his brother, Hugh, who was a subscribing shareholder (8 sixty-fourths), along with his eldest brother, John (4 sixty-fourths). In all there were 14 shareholders – 3 mariners, 2 shipbuilders, 6 farmers, 1 carrier, 1 gentleman and a merchant from London. The following year, in 1832, Ebenezer was married and he purchased the 8 shares which his brother Hugh held. In February 1835 Ebenezer relinquished the captaincy of the *Eleanor and Jane*, selling his 8 shares to the new master, Lewis Roberts of Fron, Nefyn. During the same year the 66 ton schooner, *Ebenezer*, was launched from the stocks at Nefyn and Ebenezer Parry was the subscribing owner and master with a 12 sixty-fourths shareholding. Both his brothers were also shareholders, along with 6 other Nefyn folk plus a shopkeeper from Edern and 3 Liverpool residents. By 1845 Ebenezer also owned 4 shares in his brother John's schooner, *Vron*, and in 1854 he purchased 2 additional shares in the Ebenezer from one of the Liverpool shareholders. After the *Ebenezer* was lost in 1859, Ebenezer Parry purchased the 110 ton brigantine *Rebecca*, recently built at Prince Edward Island, Canada, and he insured it for £900. The Parry family owned all the shares in the *Rebecca*, Ebenezer owning 40 shares and two of his sons owning the remainder.

Investments in ships usually formed the most valuable single asset a Nefyn shareholder owned at the time of his death, as the following inventories show:-

1. Inventory of Hugh Ellis, mariner, Y Maes Nefyn made 30th November 1824.[2]

His wearing apparel	£1 – 0 – 0
One sixteenth of sloop *Arvonia*	£11 – 0 – 0 (This was his brother's vessel)
One sixteenth of sloop *Dove*	£7 – 0 – 0 (Hugh was master of this vessel)

2. Inventory of Hugh Roberts, mariner, Nefyn made on 15th March, 1827[3].

His purse and apparel	£105 – 0 – 0
Household goods	£28 – 0 – 0
Shares in vessels	£312 – 0 – 0

3. Inventory of John Prichard, formerly blacksmith, latterly yeomen farmer, drawn up on 13th May 1836[4].

His apparel	£2 – 10 – 0
One horse	£3 – 10 – 0
One old cow	£3 – 0 – 0

House furniture	£10 – 5 – 6
Plough & implements	£2 – 0 – 0
4 sixty-fourths of sloop	
Lady Newborough	£20 – 0 – 0

By the mid 19th century some Nefyn inhabitants owned shares in a great many vessels. Some of the wealthier and more influential Nefyn ship owners owned and managed sizeable fleets of the newer larger North American-built sailing ships which were a more profitable investment, since they were comparatively cheaper to buy than locally-built vessels. At this time the major Nefyn ship owners were Captain John Thomas (Iorwerth Villa), John Roberts (Tan y Bryn, Morfa Nefyn), John Baugh Jarrett (Vron Oleu), Owen Griffiths (Plas), Robert Rees (Penllel, Morfa Nefyn), Captain William Thomas (Bodlondeb) and Captain William Thomas (Ty'n y Coed).

According to the Merchant Navy List of 1881 there were 57 vessels owned and managed at Nefyn during that year. There was one cutter, 5 sloops, 4 smacks and 1 flat (all between 30 and 47 tons); there were 3 brigs, 1 barquentine and 29 schooners (mostly 70 – 100 tons); and there were 2 fully rigged ships and 11 barques (519 – 1133 tons). 21 of these vessels were built at Nefyn or Porth Dinllaen; 11 were built in Canada and the remainder were built in other Welsh or English shipyards.

In 1875 a co-operative ship ownership venture on a grand scale was launched at Nefyn – the North Wales Shipping Company. Some people who had previously invested in locally-built wooden sailing ships and those built in North America now purchased shares in the *Eivion* and the *Gwynedd*, two iron barques, specially built for the new company in County Durham. All the leading Nefyn ship owners were significant shareholders in this company. In fact, 45% of all the shares were owned by ship owners, shipbuilders and bankers, while 23% were owned by quarrymen and farmers. Other investors included ministers of religion, schoolteachers, tradesmen, shopkeepers, master mariners, widows and spinsters. The company aspired to attract £200,000 in capital but only about £20,000 was actually raised. The company offices were at 2 Marine Terrace on the Morfa Road and the company secretary was Captain William Thomas, Bodlondeb.

Clearly the company was under capitalised and furthermore, by this time the economic climate in the shipping world had started to deteriorate. In 1887 the company was wound up and 2 new shipping companies were founded, the Ship Eivion Company and the Ship Gwynedd Company. The barques *Eivion* and *Gwynedd* were sold to the two newly-formed companies for £7 per ton, a considerable loss to the investors in the North Wales Shipping Company. The two new companies fared no better than their predecessor, and it was not long before they were also wound up and their two barques sold again, this time to Robert Thomas and Co. of Liverpool.

In 1884 another Nefyn shipping company was established – the Prydain Steamship Company. Capital of £32,000 was raised by issuing 320 shares at £100 each, and a new steamer, *Prydain*, was purchased. But this venture did not succeed either, for in 1896 the Prydain Steamship Company was dissolved and the *SS Prydain* was sold off.

Therefore, just before the dawn of the 20th century, the Nefyn dream of investing in locally-owned and managed ships was over. The maritime bubble had finally burst. The establishment of the large Nefyn-based shipping companies, funded by local capital, was a bold attempt to promote local ship ownership on a grander scale. That these companies failed cannot be attributed to poor company management. It was predominantly the overproduction of ships in the 1880's, combined with the recession in the shipping industry and in trade generally, which had effectively put an end to those lofty aspirations. Nevertheless, Nefyn investors and ship owners had enjoyed some good times in the past, and great credit must be given to the inhabitants of Nefyn in the 19th century for their confidence, enterprise and endeavour in the business of owning and managing ships.

(1) Beaumaris Shipping Register XR3/1825 Entry No. 3
(2) Letter of Administration re. Hugh Ellis of Nefyn B/1825/150, NLW.
(3) Will of Hugh Roberts of Nefyn B/1827/
(4) Will of John Prichard of Nefyn B/1836/161, NLW.

13. THE BUSINESS OF INSURANCE

During the first half of the 19th century marine insurance was monopolised by the societies based in ports like Liverpool and London. As we have already seen, many small provincial ship owners did not insure their vessels at all, and if a ship was totally lost, such owners could face financial ruin, although many of the more affluent people with an interest in shipping invested in a number of different vessels, thereby spreading the risk.

During the middle years of the 19th century a number of local mutual marine insurance societies were established in Caernarfonshire, offering protection to ship owners within the county. In 1841 the Porthmadog Mutual Ship Insurance Society was founded to safeguard the interests of Porthmadog ship owners. In 1843 the leading figures in Pwllheli and Nefyn shipping attempted to form their own society, but the plan was inexplicably abandoned. In 1853 a Bangor society was founded and a few years later another attempt to found a marine insurance society was made by Pwllheli and Nefyn shipping interests. In 1858 the Pwllheli and Nefyn Mutual Marine Insurance Society was successfully established with offices in Nefyn.

The demand for marine insurance grew so rapidly during the 1850's and 1860's that the Pwllheli and Nefyn Society spawned other Nefyn-based 'clwbs' as they were called locally. By January 1870 there were 5 related ship insurance societies based in Nefyn – The Pwllheli and Nefyn Mutual Marine Insurance Society, The Provincial A1 Mutual Marine Insurance Society, The Provincial Shipowners' Mutual Marine Protection Society, The Ancient Briton Mutual Marine Insurance Society and The Cambrian Freight and Outfit Mutual Marine Insurance Company. Unlike the Porthmadog society, which focused almost exclusively upon Porthmadog ships, the Nefyn clubs secured business not only from Nefyn and Pwllheli but also from Caernarfon and Y Felinheli as well as from ports further afield, such as Liverpool, London, Newcastle, Glasgow and Dublin. In 1870 they insured 1104 vessels with an insurable value of £1,204,170, and those vessels included many of the larger, more expensive, ocean-going ships. The directors of the societies fell into four categories – the Nefyn directors, those from Pwllheli, others from Caernarfon and a miscellaneous group from other ports like Liverpool and London. The AGM's of the societies were always held either in Nefyn or Pwllheli.

In 1872 two more Nefyn societies were added to the list, The North Wales Mutual Marine Insurance Company Ltd and The Victoria Mutual

Marine Insurance Company Ltd. In order to cater specifically for the new large iron sailing ships being purchased by ship owners, two further clubs were established. They were called The Ancient Briton Iron Sailing Ships' Freight and Outfit Mutual Marine Insurance Association Ltd and The North and South Wales Iron Sailing Ships' Freight and Outfit Mutual Marine Insurance Association Ltd. They certainly seemed to love attaching grand titles to their societies! By 1879 there were 8 mutual marine insurance societies based in Nefyn and the value of the vessels insured within the town exceeded £2,000,000. At this time there were ship insurance offices on the Fron (J.B. Jarrett – manager and secretary), at Tan y Dderwen (Evan Jones) and at 2 Marine Terrace (William Thomas). In 1880 The Carnarvon and Nefyn Mutual Marine Insurance Association Ltd and The Carnarvon and Nefyn Shipowners' Mutual Marine Protection Society were founded, reflecting the greater role assumed by Caernarfon owners within the Nefyn societies and the diminishing interest of the Pwllheli faction, whose shipping interests had recently become more closely associated with Porthmadog.

The 1880's was a period marked by a deepening depression and a decline in the need for sailing vessels. Coastal trading had been hit by the growing importance of the railways, while the overproduction of ships, the preference for steam power and the recession in foreign trade generally seriously affected the Nefyn societies. Therefore many of the larger sailing vessels began to be withdrawn from the books of these local insurance 'clubs'. The number of vessels insured with the Nefyn clubs continued to decline steadily and by 1885 only 303 vessels, with an aggregate insurance value of £764,530, were covered at Nefyn. By 1890 the Nefyn societies had ceased to exist, apart from the Provincial society and the 'Carnarvon and Nefyn' association, both of which continued to operate until 1901.

It is remarkable that a small town on the northern coast of the Llŷn peninsula should have become an important centre for ship insurance, and that it should have attracted business from some of the major ports in Britain. The story of the Nefyn clubs is a reflection of the confident, buoyant attitude which existed in Nefyn during the second half of the 19th century and it stands as a testimony to the vigour and commercial skill of some of the leading maritime figures within the town.

A type of local insurance which began earlier in Nefyn and which survived longer was the friendly society, by which folk could insure themselves against sickness and death upon payment of an annual subscription. The earliest Nefyn friendly society was Clwb Mawr founded in 1827 by John Roberts (Bwlch Glas), William Evans (Tan y

Maes), Hugh Davies (Tŷ Clap) and Henry Jones (Holborn). At first it was based in the house of John Roberts, until in 1846 they built their own clubhouse at Y Maes. For many years this clubhouse was also rented out for use as a day school, a navigational school and a place of worship for the Particular Baptists. The Clwb Mawr club house still stands at Y Maes and is now used as storehouse.

Another local friendly society was the Madryn Lodge which was founded in the 1830's and which was a branch of the Oddfellows. Among its founders were John Griffith and William Griffith of Nefyn and Hugh Davies of Edern. Hugh Davies, the nailer of Stryd y Llan, Nefyn became its secretary. Another society, Cymdeithas y Morwyr, was formed in 1839. Incorporated by Act of Parliament as the Shipwrecked Mariners' Society, membership was open to all sailors and fishermen upon payment of an annual fee of 3 shillings.

One of the highlights of the Nefyn calendar each year used to be the Christmas Day parade of Clwb Mawr and the Madryn Lodge. Members of each society would march in procession to Morfa Nefyn, decked out in their regalia. The Nefyn town band marched at the head of the Madryn Lodge, while the Clwb Mawr was led by the Llanrug band. At Morfa Nefyn the Clwb Mawr and Madryn Lodge would meet up with the Edern Club (Cymdeithas Gyfallgar Edern), which was accompanied by the Nantlle band. This procession must have been quite a spectacle for the crowds which turned out to watch it!

14. WRECKS AND RESCUES

The northern coastline of Llŷn consists of precipitous cliffs and headlands, at the foot of which is a rocky shoreline, interspersed with sandy bays and beaches. As this coast faces the westerly prevailing winds, the seas here can be particularly inhospitable, especially when the winter gales blow. It has already been mentioned that in former times this coastline was busy with an assortment of coastwise traffic to and from the ports north and south of Caernarfon Bay. Therefore it is not surprising that a great number of sailing vessels foundered on this coast. As early as 1804 Thomas Rogers, an engineer working on plans to improve Porth Dinllaen harbour, referred to the many wrecks occurring along these shores.

As the coasting traffic grew year on year, so the number of wrecked vessels increased. A notable shipwreck occurred in January 1839 when the brig *Sappho*, carrying West Indian molasses, got into difficulties in Caernarfon Bay. For many hours the ship's captain and his crew struggled to save the vessel. As night fell the captain, realising that there was little hope of avoiding disaster, gave to each crew member 2 gold sovereigns to be sewn into his pocket. This money was intended to cover the cost of burial if their bodies were washed up on the shore. In the middle of the night the *Sappho* was driven onto the rocks where she broke up rapidly. Only one crew member survived, a boy who was found upon the shore the next morning asleep in an empty molasses barrel. The bodies of the rest of the crew were subsequently washed ashore and were buried in Nefyn churchyard.

Other wrecks followed. In 1863 the Receiver of Wrecks reported that, during the previous 25 years, a total of 206 vessels had been wrecked in the Nefyn/Porth Dinllaen area with considerable loss of life. In December of the same year, several vessels were sheltering in the bay as a ferocious storm battered the coast. Some of the vessels dragged their anchors and were driven ashore. A local man, Robert Rees of Morfa Nefyn with a rope tied round his waist and assisted by 4 others, managed to save a total of 28 lives. For his outstanding bravery he was awarded a Board of Trade bronze medal and the thanks of the RNLI on vellum.

As yet there was no lifeboat stationed along the northern coast of Llŷn, although there were stations at Llanddwyn (at the entrance to the Menai Strait), Abersoch and Porthmadog (both on the southern coast). The report of the Receiver of Wrecks and the dramatic rescue by Robert Rees were undoubtedly instrumental in finally persuading the RNLI to establish a lifeboat station at Porth Dinllaen in 1864. During the same year, a Board of Trade life-saving apparatus post was established at Morfa Nefyn, consisting of a horse-drawn wagon, containing various items of rescue equipment including a shore to ship rocket-propelled line. The building, built to house this equipment, can still be seen near the children's playground in Morfa Nefyn.

In the period between the two world wars the Coastguard Service established a lookout post on the headland overlooking the bay and three coastguard cottages were built adjoining the golf course, although these are now used as holiday cottages. However, the Coastguard Rescue Service still operates from Porth Dinllaen. It consists of several volunteers, trained and skilled in cliff rescue, and a 4 wheel drive vehicle equipped with a host of safety and rescue equipment. When necessary they work in conjunction with the local lifeboat and with Search and Rescue helicopters from R.A.F. Valley on Anglesey.

Altogether eight lifeboats have served at Porth Dinllaen since the station was opened. The first 4 boats (the *Cotton Shepperd* (1864-77), two lifeboats called *George Moore* (1877-88 & 1888-1902) and the *Barbara Fleming* (1902-26) were all self-righting boats with 10 or 12 oars. The next vessel (called M.O.Y.E. 1926-49) was a Watson class self-righter with a petrol-driven engine. The 2 lifeboats which followed, the *Charles Henry Ashley* (1949-79) and the *Kathleen Mary* (1979-87), were Watson class boats each with 2 diesel engines. The present lifeboat, the *Hetty Rampton* (1987-present day) is a 'Tyne' class self-righting vessel with 2 very powerful diesel engines.

Some idea of the arduous and dangerous work undertaken by oarsmen in the rowing lifeboats of the 19th and early 20th centuries may be glimpsed from the events of 18th January 1881. At lunchtime on that day, during one of the worst storms in living memory and in freezing conditions, the first *George Moore* was launched to aid an Abersoch fishing smack that was dragging her anchors and drifting helplessly in violent seas. With immense difficulty the oarsmen battled their way to the smack and manoeuvred alongside to rescue the crew of 3. Within a short time the smack's anchor chain snapped and she was driven ashore. After several hours of strenuous rowing, the lifeboat crew finally managed to struggle back to their station with their rescued charges. At 7.30 p.m. that same evening as the lifeboatmen were still recovering from their first ordeal, they were summoned once more to rescue the crew of a Caernarfon schooner which had been driven on to the rocks, off Penrhyn Nefyn. After an exhausting struggle, the lifeboatmen managed to row to the schooner and rescue its crew of 5 and, in the early hours of the following morning, the crew of the lifeboat (which had been damaged on the rocks) managed to return to station. After 5 hours of continuous rowing through stormy seas, they arrived back at their base thoroughly fatigued.

Whilst the first 4 Porth Dinllaen lifeboats were required to go to the assistance of schooners, smacks and small steamers, more recent rescues have tended to feature people engaged in leisure pursuits – swimmers, shore walkers, wind surfers, sea anglers, and people in yachts, dinghies, speedboats and inflatables.

In August 1951 at 10.10 p.m. the *Charles Henry Ashley* was called out to search for a missing yacht. On a very dark night and in rough seas, after nearly 3 hours of searching, the yacht was spotted at anchor off Porth O'er, sheltering close to the rocky shoreline. With great difficulty and in the face of tremendous danger to both the lifeboat and the yacht, the coxswain managed to manoeuvre his vessel between the yacht and the rocks to rescue the 3 yachtsmen. The lifeboat had been at sea for nearly 8 hours before she was able to return safely to station with the three rescued sailors. For his outstanding courage and seamanship the Porth Dinllaen Coxswain was awarded the RNLI Silver Medal and the Mechanic received the Institution's Thanks on Vellum. Each member of the lifeboat crew was granted an additional cash payment.

On August 31st 1976 the *Charles Henry Ashley* was involved in the heroic rescue of a boy trapped in the dark 80 feet up the cliff at Porth y Nant, north east of Nefyn and another boy trapped at the foot of the cliffs. The lifeboat was launched at 11.15 p.m., but when it arrived at the scene the Coxswain was unable to take his boat between the rocks at the bottom of the cliffs. Second Coxswain John Scott and Lifeboatman Glyn Roberts, using a small boarding boat, managed to negotiate the rocks in an 8 foot swell to reach the foot of the cliffs. Taking off his sea boots and his thick woollen socks, and illuminated by the lifeboat's powerful searchlight, Lifeboatman Roberts climbed the almost sheer cliff face to reach the lad. During the descent, when they were about 30 feet from the bottom, Lifeboatman Roberts slipped and fell on to the rocks below. Despite being cut, bruised and badly shaken, he climbed up once more to reach the lad and bring him down to safety. Both boys were then helped into the small boat and the Second Coxswain had to use all his skill to negotiate the rocks once more in order bring his small craft back to the lifeboat. For his outstanding bravery Lifeboatman Roberts was awarded the RNLI Bronze Medal and was subsequently given an award for the most courageous RNLI rescue of 1976. Second Coxswain John Scott received the Institution's Thanks on Vellum for his fine seamanship.

So far, 1 Silver Medal and 3 Bronze Medals have been awarded to Porth Dinllaen lifeboatmen. RNLI Letters of Thanks on Vellum have been sent to Porth Dinllaen on 5 separate occasions and additional monetary awards have been made to the crew 4 times. In 1978 the Porth Dinllaen Hon. Sec. was made an Honorary Life Governor of the RNLI, the highest award made to a voluntary member, and in 1990 Coxswain, Griffith Jones, was awarded the British Empire Medal in the Queen's New Year's Honours List. At the time of writing the Porth Dinllaen lifeboats have been launched on 502 occasions and a total of 364 lives have been saved. These figures are evidence of the Porth Dinllaen lifeboat's proud record, and to this day its crews of volunteer local men continue the selfless tradition of risking their own lives whilst going to the aid of people exposed to danger off the northern coast of Llŷn.

15. NEFYN-OWNED SHIPS

Whilst it is known that, at the time of Elizabeth I, Nefyn and Porth Dinllaen had no vessels of their own apart from fishing boats, both ports certainly possessed some small trading vessels during the early 17th century. But it was during the 18th and 19th centuries that Nefyn developed into a port and a shipping centre of some importance in North Wales. The purpose of this section is to take an overview of the broad trends in Nefyn shipping and to cover in greater detail certain vessels owned and managed at Nefyn.

During the 18th century the ships owned at Nefyn were principally sloops which were the little vessels carrying all manner of cargoes around the coasts of Britain. They exported slates, herrings and farm produce and they brought in commodities like shop goods, limestone, salt, timber and coal.

The earliest Beaumaris Shipping Register 1786-1818 contains the details of 48 sloops and 3 brigantines with Nefyn owners. These vessels were all locally built by Welsh shipbuilders, mainly at Pwllheli, Nefyn and Porth Dinllaen, but also at Caernarfon, Cricieth, Barmouth and Aberystwyth. Early sloops such as the 19 ton *Sea Horse*, built at Barmouth in 1754, were relatively small. Gradually sloops became larger in size like the 44 ton *Prosperity* built at Pwllheli in 1798 and the 73 ton *Arvonia* built at Nefyn in 1813.

Like so many local sloops during the 18th and early 19th centuries, the 37 ton *Brunswick*, built at Pwllheli in 1794 and owned by John Jones of Nefyn, mariner, Griffith Jones, merchant and Ann Jones, spinster, both of Pistyll, was engaged in the Ffestiniog slate trade. With Hugh Ellis of Mursefer, Nefyn as master, on 14th March 1803 the *Brunswick* was loading slates at Ynys Cyngar in the Glaslyn Estuary, but in 1809 this vessel went missing without trace of vessel or crew. A typical early 19th century sloop owned at Nefyn was the 47 ton *Eleanor and Jane*, built at Cricieth by John Roberts in 1814. This was a square- stemmed vessel with one deck and one mast, no galley and no figure head. She was 46ft 11ins long by 16ft 2ins in the beam and she had a hold height of 8ft 4ins. The *Eleanor and Jane* was lost in 1840. Of the Nefyn and Porth Dinllaen sloops on the 1786-1818 Beaumaris Shipping Register 75% were less than 40 tons.

Considerably larger than the vast majority of the sloops were the early brigantines, such as the 78 ton *Prince of Orange* (built at Nefyn in 1784), the 95 ton *Maria* (built at Porth Dinllaen in 1786) and the 101 ton *Waterloo* (built at Nefyn in 1815). The *Waterloo* was owned by several shareholders including Charles Jones, a Nefyn mariner who was also the master. She was 69ft 7ins long with a beam of 18ft 6ins and a hold height of 10ft 8ins. On 21st March 1855, while sailing from King's Lynn to Scheidam in the Netherlands with a cargo of barley, she struck a whale in fog about 50 miles off Lowestoft. The crew were forced to abandon ship and 20 minutes later the vessel capsized and sank. The crew were subsequently rescued by a French fishing boat and landed safely at Calais.

In the second quarter of the 19th century two-masted schooners began to appear. The 84 ton *Catherine* was built at Nefyn in 1821 by John Thomas for Hugh Roberts of Nefyn. Hugh Roberts was also the master and in 1881 the *Catherine* was still owned at Nefyn by Richard Williams of Pool St. In 1882 she was in collision with an Isle of Man vessel and sank. By 1850 the two-masted schooner was the most popular coasting vessel. Schooners up to about 100 tons were now sailing the coasts of Britain, trading with the Baltic, the Mediterranean and even crossing the Atlantic to the eastern seaboard of North America. The *Jane and Ellen* was a schooner of 80 tons, built by H. Roberts of Nefyn in 1839 for William Parry of Nefyn. In 1865 she was involved in a collision with the steamer Emma and awarded £396 in damages. In 1879 she became stranded in the Menai Strait, while on passage from Llanaelhaearn to Runcorn with a cargo of stone. She was finally condemned and broken up at Y Felinheli in 1892.

As the sloop began to decline as a coaster in favour of the two-masted schooner certain sloops were lengthened and converted into schooners, although some Nefyn-owned sloops continued to sail throughout the 19th century. One or two sloops continued to be built like the 38 ton *Elizabeth* built at Trefriw in 1847 and the *Eliza, Ann and Ellen*, built at Pwllheli in 1854, both of which were still sailing in 1881. Furthermore, a few of the early sloops, like the *Amity* of Nefyn, continued to operate well into the second half of the 19th century. The *Amity* was a 34 ton sloop built at Pwllheli in 1809 and she spent many years transporting limestone from Caernarfon and Liverpool to Porth Dinllaen and Nefyn. She also carried granite setts from Llanaelhaearn to Merseyside. In 1825 the master and part owner was John Roberts of Nefyn. In 1838 William Howell of Penisa'r dre, Nefyn, was the master and majority shareholder. After William Howell's death he was succeeded by his eldest son, John William Howell. On 14th September 1872, while crossing Llandudno Bay with a cargo of setts from Llanaelhaearn bound for Liverpool, the vessel sprang a leak and started to sink. John William Howell, the master, and his mate abandoned ship, which subsequently sank. The *Amity* had sailed for an incredible 63 years, and during most of that period she carried very heavy punishing cargoes.

Generally, sloops were not adorned with a figurehead, but from the late 1830's many vessels began to be fitted with such carved wooden embellishments at the prow. Most figureheads were either the busts of male or female figures or the full length carving of a man, a youth or a girl, and some of these representations were very elaborate and decorative. For example, Evan Griffith's (Stryd y Ffynnon) schooner *Revival*, built at Porth Dinllaen in 1859, had the figurehead of a preacher with an open Bible in his hands. Such adornments were an indication of the increasing pride which owners were taking in the appearance of their vessels.

Square riggers were increasingly deployed by Nefyn owners from about the end of the first quarter of the 19th century. The 91 ton brig *Zebra* was built at Nefyn in 1825 by John John Thomas for Hugh Williams of Pistyll, who was washed overboard and drowned near Yr Eifl. The *Zebra* was subsequently owned by Evan Williams of Tai'rlon, Nefyn. She traded around the coasts of the British Isles, with occasional visits to continental ports like Hamburg and Harburg. She was eventually stranded at Ballyquinton Point, Ireland on 19th September 1885 and became a total wreck.

The *Ardent* was a brig of 105 tons built and owned by John Thomas of Nefyn in 1826. In 1844 she was practically rebuilt and her tonnage increased. She was 71 ft long 20 ft. in the beam and had a hold height of 12 ft. She was later sold to Robert Jones of Nefyn. In 1858 Captain Robert Jones, sought shelter at Milford for several days during a severe gale. Eventually he decided to leave the safety of Milford Haven before the storm had abated, but this was a grave mistake and the following day the *Ardent* was lost with all hands.

From about the middle of the 19th century the vessels operated by Nefyn owners were fewer in number but generally they were larger in size and tonnage. Locally-built two-masted schooners which came into service tended to be about 100 tons or slightly larger. The 132 ton schooner *Commodore* was built at Nefyn in 1844 by Hugh Roberts, who was also the owner. In the 1870's she was owned by H. Parry of Nefyn but was lost under his command off Swanage in 1877. The *Frances Ann* was a schooner of 99 tons built by James Owen at Porth Dinllaen in 1862 for John Thomas of Nefyn. She was 79 ft 1in long, 22ft 3ins in the beam with a hold height of 10ft 6ins. Later the *Frances Ann* was sold to a Caernarfon owner and she was lost off Bovers Head in 1873. One of the larger two-masted schooners was the 127 ton *Miss Thomas*, built by Robert Thomas at Porth Nefyn in 1864 for John Thomas of Nefyn. She was 80ft long with a beam of 21ft 6ins and a hold height of 11ft 8ins. She traded in the Baltic, the Elbe and along the coast of Morocco. During one voyage into the Baltic she was driven ashore in a storm and had to be rekeeled at Landskrona, Sweden. She was finally lost in the River Thames on 16th November1896.

The only three-masted schooner to be built at Nefyn was the 193 ton *Ebenezer Parry* built by Griffith Owen in 1877 for Captain Henry Parry of Mursefer, Stryd y Ffynnon. Her dimensions were 100ft 6ins by 24ft 6ins and a hold height of 13ft 2ins. She traded with ports in the Mediterranean, Scandinavia and the Baltic, the eastern seaboard of North and South America (e.g. New York, Rosario, Frey Bentos and Port Natal, Brazil) and ports along the Spanish Main. About 1890-1 she was sold to Pwllheli owners and later she was resold to Porthmadog, and re-registered as the *Ellen Lloyd*. Her rig was altered to a barquentine and she was deployed on the fish trade between Newfoundland and Europe. In about 1912 she was sold to Cornwall but was subsequently bought by French owners and renamed the *Robert Marguerite*. She was eventually sunk at Le Havre in about 1917.

There were also several locally built square riggers owned at Nefyn during the second half of the 19th century. They included the brigs *Anna and Mary* (175 tons built at Nefyn in 1856), the *Linus* (189 tons built at Nefyn in 1857) and the *Simon* (225 tons built at Nefyn in 1860); the brigantine *Nanhoron* (147 tons built at Nefyn in 1859); and the barque *Isolina* (390 tons built at Nefyn 1866), the largest vessel to leave the stocks at Nefyn. The *Linus* was built by Robert Thomas for John Roberts of Nefyn. She was 105ft 6ins long and 22ft 7ins in the beam with a hold height of 13ft 5ins. She was notable for being one of the fastest vessels in the region. She was eventually sold to Porthmadog owners and was converted to a barquentine. In 1901 she was sold to Lerwick in the Shetlands and was still afloat after World War II. In 1892 she made the 6000 mile voyage to the River Plate with a cargo of slates, returning home with phosphate from Aruba. On another occasion she sailed round Cape Horn to Peru. The barque *Isolina* was also built by Robert Thomas. She was 138ft long with 27ft beam and a hold height of 16ft 5ins. She was damaged during her launching and had to go to Holyhead for repairs. In 1874 she was sold to owners at Falmouth.

From the mid 19th century more North American-built vessels were owned at Nefyn because they were well-constructed and cheaper to purchase than locally-built ships. At first Nefyn owners purchased schooners such as the *Rebecca* (110 tons built at Prince Edward Island in 1859) and the *Mercy Jane* (60 tons built in Nova Scotia). Soon the wealthier Nefyn ship owners began to buy large square-rigged Canadian-built barques like the *Pontiac* (608 tons built Quebec in 1860), *Fairy Belle* (519 tons built New Brunswick in 1863), *Wandering Sprite* (781 tons built

Quebec in 1868), the J.P. Smith (772 tons built Quebec in 1869) the *Medusa* (760 tons built Nova Scotia in 1870) *Saigon* (768 tons built Quebec 1871) and *Felicitas* (754 tons built Quebec 1874). There were also Canadian-built fully rigged ships such as the *Lakefield* (997 tons built Quebec in 1875).

Finally in the late 1870's Nefyn ship owners and investors turned their attention to British-built iron sailing vessels, for the cost of iron and steel had fallen and it was found that iron ships were more cost effective because they could be built larger and therefore were able to carry a greater tonnage of cargo than wooden ships. As mentioned previously, the barques *Gwynedd* (1953 tons) and *Eivion* (1133 tons) both built at Hylton, County Durham, were the two vessels owned at Nefyn by the North Wales Shipping Company.

The names given to ships were many and varied. Many local vessels were named after relatives of an owner (e.g. *Eleanor and Catherine, John and Mary, Margaret Parry, Hugh Roberts*). Others were named after the relative of a valued foreign customer (e.g. *Walter Ulric, Minnie Elkan, Clara Felicia*). Some ships were named after royalty (*Prince of Orange, George IV*), well known local folk (*Lord Newborough*) or historical figures (*Hannibal, Magellan*). Some names reflected family relationships (*Brothers, Two Sisters*) or local place names (*Nefyn, Nanhoron, Vron, Bardsey*), while other vessels bore the names of creatures (*Sea Horse, Pelican, Reindeer, Pilot Fish*). Some ships' names reflected their owners' aspirations (*Prosperity, New Hope, Providence*) or personal qualities (*Perseverence, Resolution, Amiable*). Certain ships were named after precious jewels (*Emerald, Pearl*) while others had a mythological flavour (*Phoenix, Mermaid, Medusa*).

The number of crew on board a ship obviously varied according to the size of the vessel. A sloop such as the 28 ton *Amity* was manned by a crew of 2 or 3, consisting of a master, a mate and sometimes a boy. A 78 ton schooner like the *Vron* had a master, a mate and 3 other crew members. A large 3-masted schooner such as the 193 ton *Ebenezer Parry* sailed with a master, a mate, and 6 ordinary crew members. The 1133 ton iron barque *Eivion*, on one of its voyages in 1891/2, carried a master, a mate, a second mate, and 13 additional members of crew.

Some Nefyn ships were altered during the course of their sailing careers. Some were enlarged by inserting a complete new middle section. Rigs were altered – sloops were converted into schooners, schooners were changed into brigs or brigantines, and brigs were altered into barquentines. Some Nefyn vessels ended their days as river barges - the *Revival* was re-registered in 1908 as a Mersey river boat, having had its masts removed.

Throughout the 19th century ships were the lifeblood of communities like Nefyn. They were the means by which many Nefyn men earned their livelihood. For large numbers of other local folk, investment in locally-owned vessels brought the prospect of additional income. Moreover, local ships provided important lines of communication with the outside world, for they were the means by which essential goods were imported into the area and by which locally produced commodities were exported. Nefyn ships not only contributed enormously to the economy of the local community but also to the wealth of Caernarfonshire and North Wales generally. Today the weather vane in the shape of a sailing ship, situated on top of the old St Mary's Church tower, is a constant reminder of the vital part which sailing vessels formerly played in the life of this maritime town.

16. NEFYN SEA CAPTAINS AND SAILORS

The Nefyn records (the Parish Registers, monumental inscriptions, wills, directories etc) as well as the maritime records (Beaumaris Shipping Registers and Crew Lists and Agreements) are packed with the details of Nefyn mariners and sea captains, and it has been said that the little town of Nefyn produced more mariners for its size than any other place in Britain. The monumental inscriptions in the 4 graveyards within the parish bear witness to the large number of seafarers who lived here. Recorded on Nefyn tombstones are the names of 252 Nefyn men identified as sea captains with a further 84 detailed as sailors, the earliest inscription bearing the date 1808. But it must be remembered that the families of many ordinary sailors were too poor to afford a headstone and so their loved ones lie in unmarked graves. Furthermore, large numbers of mariners were lost at sea and so for them there is no record among the gravestones.

The excellent Welsh Mariners Index website records the names of 660 mariners born in Nefyn. But even these figures represent just the tip of the iceberg, since this site does not include several individuals known to have been Nefyn-born mariners and it records very few sailors born before 1800.

On the 1851 Census Return, out of a total adult male population of 474, 86 are recorded as mariners or master mariners. A further 66 were certainly away at sea on the night of the census, for their wives are entered as 'Mariner's Wife' or Master Mariner's Wife', and so that makes a total of 152 known mariners/master mariners residing in Nefyn in 1851. But this figure does not represent the total number of Nefyn seafarers at that time. Bachelor mariners and unmarried sons who were away at sea on the night of the census (of whom there must have been many) cannot be accounted for on that document. Therefore, although it is impossible to estimate the total number of Nefyn seamen in 1851, it is almost certainly true that more Nefyn men earned their livelihood at sea than by any other occupation. The other main area of employment in the mid 19th century was agriculture with 156 Nefyn men recorded as being associated with farming.

Who were these men who spent their lives sailing the seas? Originally they were the sons of fishermen, farmers, tradesmen and labourers. Later there developed a tradition of seafaring within many families, sons following fathers to sea so that generations of the same families became mariners. Many sailors began their careers at sea as boys, some as young as 12 or 13 years old. At first they joined the sloops and small schooners engaged in coastal trading, perhaps joining a vessel of which a relative or family friend was master. From such 'old hands' they learned the skills of seamanship and many became masters themselves, sailing vessels in which they had become part or sole owners. Later on, young seamen joined the large ocean-going, three-masted schooners and barques which sailed all over the world. Many went on to become fully qualified master mariners having passed their Board of Trade examinations and obtained their certificates of competence.

It is amazing that so many should have been willing to suffer the rigours and dangers of a life at sea for such a poor wage. In the late 1890's the monthly pay for an Ordinary Seaman ranged from £1 to £2 5s 0d, while a boy earned 10 shillings per month. Although generally speaking, sailors engaged in the coastal trade enjoyed better food and more frequent periods on land, the dangers of the rocky coastal routes were considerable, frequently resulting in the loss of a sloop or a schooner with all hands. The following few examples illustrate the heavy price paid by some Nefyn mariners sailing the British coastline in small vessels. Richard Parry, aged 24, master of the *Endeavour*, was drowned when he fell overboard near Yr Eifl on 25th September 1831. Captain Henry Parry, master of the schooner *Margaret Parry*, was lost together with his entire crew in 1848 when the vessel went down in the Irish Sea while on passage from Chester to Londonderry. Captain William Parry, aged 53, was accidentally drowned at Poole on 11th February 1853. Captain Robert Jones, master of the *Ardent*, was drowned off Milford Haven when his vessel went down with all hands during a violent storm. Captain Robert Jones, the 76 year old master of the *Four Brothers*, was lost together with his crew when his ship sank in the bay at Conwy on 29th December 1860. The following day, Captain Robert Hughes, aged 58, died at Portsmouth and was buried in a cemetery in that town. Captain Ellis Jones of Stryd y Llan and a 13 year old Nefyn crew member called Richard Jones, were lost when the sloop *Leeba* went missing without trace off Milford Haven in March 1866 while transporting a cargo of culm from Neath to Pwllheli. Captain Henry Roberts, aged 48 and 13 year old John Jones of Y Maes were drowned when the schooner *Henry Catherine* was shipwrecked at Porth Neigwl on 5th December 1866 on a return voyage from Dublin. Evan Davies, Y Maes, was drowned when the schooner *Angler* was lost with all hands in St Georges Channel while on passage from Sunderland to Dublin on 18th February 1868.

Men sailing in ocean-going ships fared no better. They could be away from home for long periods (sometimes up to 3 years as we have already seen), their food was often poor and monotonous, many foreign ports were ravaged by disease and the oceans could be particularly dangerous during violent stormy weather. John Owen of Cefn Y Maes aged 20, was killed when he fell from the mizzen mast of the barque *William Owen* on 12th October 1870. Evan Jones, Wint, died in Calcutta on 24th October 1885 aged 21. John Roberts of Wern was lost at sea in 1887. Robert Griffith aged 16 of Cerniog Bach, was drowned on a voyage from Australia to England on 23rd May 1888. Evan Ebenezer Parry of Stryd y Ffynnon, mate on the *Edwin*, went missing without trace in March 1891 while the vessel was docked at Genoa, and an inquiry subsequently concluded that he had accidentally fallen into the harbour and drowned, although his body was never recovered. Hugh Williams, aged 19, died in Rio de Janeiro in September 1891. Captain William Williams died in Penang on 11th May 1894 aged 48. Captain D D Jones of the *Cambrian Queen* died in Havana on 24th June 1897 aged 31. Four Nefyn seamen, including the two sons of Mr. & Mrs. Jones, Penpalment, Nefyn, died on board the *S.S. North Anglia* during a violent storm in the Bay of Biscay in 1922. Captain William Meredith was lost when the *Annie Thomas* sank with all hands during a voyage from Cardiff to Acapulco with a cargo of coal. Captain William Davies, Craig y Mor and master of the *Monkbarns*, died at Rio de Janeiro in February 1926 during his last voyage before retirement.

Many mariners from the parish perished during the 2 World Wars. Among that number were the following: Lieutenant Evan H. Williams, R.N.R. Tŷ Canol aged 30, died when *HMS Hampshire* was sunk in June 1916, the same disaster in which Lord Kitchener was drowned. Master Griffith Owen aged 45 and Carpenter William Williams , both of Morfa lost their lives when their ship 'The North Wales' was torpedoed off the Scillies in October 1916. Three Morfa seamen (Boatswain William Thomas aged 50, his son 19 year old Hugh Thomas, and Seaman Hugh David Owen aged 23) were all lost when the *S.S. Canganian* was sunk off the Scottish coast in November 1916. Captain Evan Jones, Bryn Beuno aged 59 lost his life when his vessel was sunk by enemy action on 23rd May 1917. Captain Richard Griffith, Llysarborth, died when his ship *S.S Semantha* was torpedoed in 1917 in the Mediterranean, while transporting munitions to the troops in the Middle East. During World War II Hugh Williams, Gwynfryn was lost during an Arctic passage, carrying supplies to North Russia, as was Captain William Williams of Morfa. Thomas David Davies 'Isfryn' was killed when his ship was targeted by a German U boat in the Dutch Antilles and 24 year old Idris Jones of Morfa lost his life when his convoy was attacked by U boats in 1941 while en route to Gibraltar.

Other Nefyn men fared better. Although his ship, the *Conway Castle* was sunk by the German cruiser Dresden in 1915, Captain John Williams

'Min y Mor' managed to survive and was able to give the navy such detailed information that they were able to locate and destroy the enemy cruiser. For this action Captain Williams was mentioned in despatches. Captain Owen 'Bay View' Nefyn was decorated for his skill in managing to escape the persistent attentions of a German U boat.

It was not only the sailors and sea captains who suffered as a result of a life at sea. The wives and children of seafarers endured long periods of separation from husbands and fathers. In 1836 the curate of Nefyn stated that the children of the parish were disorderly because their fathers were frequently away at sea and they lacked "the advantage of paternal control"[1]. Wives not only had to bring up the children but they also had to tend to the gardens and plots of land. Relatives lived in constant fear of bad news and this anxiety was heightened when a ship was overdue. Henry Parry recorded that, before the First World War, Nefyn folk kept abreast of the shipping news by following the movement of vessels in the Shipping Gazette, which was displayed daily in the Gazette Room, a small room in the basement of the Madryn Hall (built in 1898, officially opened in 1899 and recently demolished). J Ifor Davies refers to Nefyn people seeking news of ships in the period between the wars in the Board of Trade reports which appeared regularly in the Journal of Commerce, copies of which were always available in the Liberal and Constitutional Clubs within the town.

Wives of master mariners, together with their young children, sometimes accompanied their men folk on voyages around the world. J Ifor Davies records how his mother, following her marriage to his father, Captain William Davies, sailed with him in the Gwydyr Castle between 1905 and 1912. By that time they had 3 children, the eldest of whom was of school age. Thus their global wanderings as a family were forced to come to an end. The pregnant wife of Captain William Thomas and his young son were sailing with him in his ship Cricieth Castle in 1912 when it sank in the South Atlantic Ocean. The family made a remarkable escape in an open ship's boat and eventually landed at Port Stanley in the Falkland Islands. Subsequently a daughter, Mercy Malvinas Thomas, was born, her name serving as a constant reminder of the family's good fortune in surviving to reach the Malvinas or Falkland Islands. Mary Ann Meredith, the wife of Captain William Meredith of Ropewalk Nefyn, was less fortunate. In 1894 whilst accompanying her husband on the Dominion, which was carrying a cargo of wheat from Tacoma, she died at sea.

Ships' captains were generally a courageous and resourceful breed of men, whose experience often seemed to have given them a sixth sense concerning the weather and impending danger. Many captains of the larger ocean-going ships also developed great skill in selecting and managing their crews, for the crew of a large three-masted schooner or barque often consisted of men from several different countries. Not only did the captain have to solicit contracts for profitable cargoes in the various ports into which the vessel sailed, but he also had to deal with matters such as mutiny, illness, injury, death at sea, the desertion and drunkenness of crew members in foreign ports of call and a host of minor misdemeanours which might occur within a motley crew. Many masters were religious and God-fearing men, who unfailingly attended divine worship when ashore. Most master mariners were Nonconformists and David Thomas records that in 1849, out of 8 trustees appointed for Capel Wesla, 5 were ships' captains. When land was purchased for the Baptist chapel in Morfa Nefyn in the mid 19th century, 2 of the 5 trustees were master mariners. The gravestone of Captain Evan Williams records that he was a deacon at the Nefyn Baptist Chapel for 38 years, and out of 61 Nefyn folk listed as subscribers to the Bible Society in 1849, 34 were ships' captains and 1 was a seaman.

Most sea captains were Liberal in their politics, and philosophical and fatalistic in their outlook on life. They were careful with money and many were teetotal, for the 'Crew Lists and Agreements' invariably included the captain's rule "No Grog", since the presence of alcohol could jeopardise the safety of both ship and crew. The majority of ships' masters invested in local shipping shares and some became quite wealthy. Many of the large houses in Nefyn were built by master mariners and, in later years, Ffordd Dewi Sant leading to Morfa Nefyn was considered the most prestigious residential area.

Having retired from going to sea, some Nefyn captains became ships' managers. Men like Ebenezer Parry and William Howell of Stryd y Ffynnon became ship's husbands to their own vessels, which were then captained by one of their sons. Others like Captain John Thomas, Iorwerth Villa, remained ashore to manage a large fleet of ships, for in 1868 he oversaw an impressive fleet of 14 vessels, and he was one of the leading Nefyn ship owners during the second half of the 19th century. Hugh Parry, born in Stryd y Ffynnon, moved to Porthmadog, the home town of his wife, and when he retired from going to sea he became one of the leading ships' agents in that port with an office on the quayside at Cornhill. Other retired Nefyn sea captains set themselves up in business, like Evan Griffiths who opened a grocer's shop in Stryd y Ffynnon, Evan Williams who opened Siop Zebra at the end of Stryd y Felin and Captain Henry Parry who ran both the Nanhoron Arms Hotel and a successful coaching business.

It was the economic recession of the 1920's which virtually brought to an end the Nefyn seafaring tradition. Large numbers of serving captains and seamen abandoned their careers at sea prematurely and sought a variety of jobs ashore. Henry Parry of Stryd y Plas took a degree in dentistry at Liverpool University and spent the rest of his working life inspecting and treating the teeth of school children on Llŷn. Captain Ellis Hugh Williams became a School Attendance Officer and eventually became the School Attendance Superintendent for Caernarfonshire. Young men also broke with tradition for they were no longer persuaded to follow their fathers and uncles into the merchant fleet. The men of Nefyn had finally turned their backs upon a working life at sea, and only a handful remained in the merchant service during the Second World War. For a while the tradition was kept alive by the large numbers of retired mariners and master mariners who lived in the town and who gathered on Y Groes in the centre of Nefyn to exchange tales of Rio, Valparaiso, Tocopilla, Durban, Hobart or rounding the Horn.

What then is the legacy of these stoical and resolute seafaring men? Because Britain is an island, the historical importance of the British merchant fleet has generally been recognised. It was from the outlying rural coastal fringes of these islands that many of the men who manned the merchant fleet were drawn, and the seafarers of Nefyn played as significant a part as any. The story of the shipmasters and seamen of Nefyn, together with their women folk, is as important as it is remarkable. All too frequently the contribution they made to the commercial prosperity of this country (often at great cost to themselves and their families) has not been fully appreciated, and there has been a lack of recognition among many historians of the part these folk played in the economic, religious, social, political and educational life of their communities. As we have seen, many ships' captains became leaders within their towns and villages. Their religious Nonconformity and Liberal political persuasion was in direct opposition to the wealthy Anglican Tory landowners who had formerly dominated local affairs, and it was a tradition which brought about a substantial change in the Welsh scene.

The sea captains and sailors who manned the sailing ships, large and small, which sailed our coasts and which voyaged to the furthest corners of the world, were an incomparable breed and they represent a way of life that has now gone for ever. The contribution they made to society both locally and nationally ought not to be undervalued, and their courage, skill and resourcefulness must never be forgotten.

(1) Report on the Borough of Nefyn 1836.

17. GRANITE QUARRYING AND BRICK MAKING

The mountains behind Nefyn and the coastal areas to the north east are comprised of Pre-Cambrian igneous rocks of a granite type called porphyry and syenite. During the 19th and early 20th centuries this stone was extensively quarried within the parish of Nefyn and the neighbouring parishes of Pistyll and Llanaelhaearn. There were several very small quarries in the Nefyn area which produced stone for local use, but much more important were the larger commercial granite quarries. They were the Gwylwyr Quarry on Mynydd Gwylwyr (the largest and most important of the Nefyn quarries), Gwaith John Lloyd and Foel Dywyrch (two quarries on Mynydd Nefyn), Tŷ Mawr or Bodeilias Quarry at Penrhyn Bodeilias (a coastal quarry at the NE extremity of the bay at Nefyn, just outside the present parish boundary), and the Moel Tŷ Gwyn Quarries known as the Vaenol and Nanhoron Quarries inside the parish of Pistyll. North east of Nefyn and strung out along the coast were other quarries – Carreg y Llam, Porth y Nant, Caer Nant and Eifl. Although these quarries lie well outside the Nefyn parish boundary, further references will be made to those which were merged into the same companies as the Nefyn quarries, while the quarry at Carreg y Llam provided work for Nefyn workers long after quarrying had ceased within Nefyn parish.

In the early 19th century Samuel Holland, who had taken over his father's slate quarrying business at Ffestiniog, saw the opportunity to make money by quarrying granite at Eifl in the parish of Llanaelhaearn. He foresaw that plenty of stone would be needed for the construction of the new harbour and town of Porth Dinllaen which was intended to become the Royal Mail packet station for Ireland. As we shall see in a later section those plans did not come to fruition. However, since large quantities of granite were also required for other purposes, the Eifl enterprise flourished and more quarries were opened along this coast.

In the late 18th/early 19th centuries the streets of the growing English industrial towns were surfaced with smooth, rounded paving or cobble stones, gathered from the beaches and exported from Porth Dinllaen and Nefyn to Merseyside, from where they were carried by canal to the towns of Lancashire, Cheshire and the Midlands. As the pace of the Industrial Revolution quickened and as the volume of heavy horse-drawn wagons with their iron-banded wheels increased, cobbles were superceded by 'setts' (small granite blocks fixed close together and sunk into the ground) because they afforded a much more even and durable road surface.

The granite quarries of the northern coast of Llŷn were essentially sett quarries, although there was also some production of lump or building stone, as well as hand-broken macadam for road building and railway ballast. Later on, huge stone crushing machines were installed in quarries like Carreg y Llam for the large scale production of road stone, railway ballast and concrete aggregates.

Work in the quarries in the early days was arduous and hazardous, and the hours were long. Bore holes for the explosives had to be drilled by human muscle-power, using a hand-held metal drill and a 5lb hammer. Men wielding sledge hammers broke the lump stone, which was then loaded by hand into wagons. Safety regulations for handling and using the explosives were inadequate, and serious accidents and fatalities were not uncommon. Settmaking was a skilled job requiring a 3–4 year apprenticeship and was therefore comparatively better paid. However, settmakers were prone to develop stooping backs in later life, owing to a working life spent in a bent position. Furthermore, quarrying was not a secure occupation for there were periods when work was scarce, especially during the winter. At such times some quarrymen went to America for extended periods to work in the quarries there. As J Ifor Davies tells, a favourite American destination for Nefyn quarry workers was Red Granite, a small township in Wisconsin. Some quarrymen made many such visits during their working lives and some settled there permanently to adopt American citizenship and become part of a thriving expatriate Welsh community in that part of the United States.

Each Nefyn quarry had its own tramway to carry the stone from the production areas to a jetty extending into the sea, where ships could tie up to receive the cargoes of stone. At the larger quarries like Gwylwyr there was an assortment of buildings including offices, a blacksmith's forge and a carpenter's workshop. Some quarrying companies also owned their own ships to transport the stone away. During their heyday the larger quarries employed a considerable workforce including a manager or foreman, rockmen to extract the rock, sledgers to break it up, platelayers to lay and repair the tramways, blacksmiths to make and repair tools and other equipment, settmakers to fashion the setts, labourers to load the stone into wagons and onto ships, and office clerks to man the offices.

The 1851 Census for Nefyn includes 58 quarry workers, of whom 9 were identified as "quarryman", 9 were described as "setts maker", 33 were referred to as "stone cutter" together with 7 younger males recorded as "apprentice" or "boy attending stone cutters". During the second half of the 19th century there was an influx into Nefyn of quarry workers from the Penmaenmawr/Llanfairfechan area and from Leicestershire. They settled permanently in the town and some of their descendants are still to be found among Nefyn residents today.

In the 1820's setts were being produced at Penmaenmawr and by 1835 the **Gwylwyr Quarry** was being worked for setts by Samuel Holland, who as we have seen was also quarrying on Yr Eifl. In 1844 Holland brought the Gwylwyr and Eifl quarries together to form the Welsh Granite Company. During the 1850's Holland's granite quarrying enterprises were acquired by Messrs Hutton and Roscoe, who also owned the vessel *Jane and Ann* of Caernarfon to transport the stone away. Another vessel called the *Geneva* was owned by John Hutton and Company.

In 1864 a company was formed to acquire the Eifl and Gwylwyr quarries together with the Tŷ Mawr quarry at Penrhyn Bodeilias. The new company was called The Welsh Granite Company Limited, with its registered offices at Yr Eifl Quarry. The Eifl and Gwylwyr quarries together were purchased for £3000 in cash and £13,000 in shares, while the plant, stores and materials at the two quarries were valued at £702 – 14s – 4d. The 1864 prospectus for the newly formed company anticipated a profit of at least £10 per cent per annum on a £32,000 investment. It emphasised the quality and durability of the granite from these quarries and stated that since 1850 60,000 paving setts had been sent from these quarries to surface the roads of Manchester, where 44 of the main streets were listed as having been paved with this material. Also included were testimonials from the authorities in Bristol, Leeds, Bangor, Wolverhampton and the War Department. Directors of the company included John Hutton as well as members of the old Tŷ Mawr Granite Company.

For many years in the 1870's and 1880's the general manager of the Welsh Granite Co Ltd was Mr. George Farron, who together with members of his family also founded the Eifl Steamship Co Ltd, which operated steamships carrying the granite away from the quarries at Gwylwyr and Eifl. This company was formed in 1883 and continued until after Farron's death in 1901.

In 1911 the Welsh Granite Co Ltd amalgamated with two quarries at Penmaenmawr (Darbishires Ltd and Brundrit & Co) to form the Penmaenmawr and Welsh Granite Co Ltd Gwylwyr now became part of a huge North Wales granite quarrying enterprise, but in terms of production and the number of men employed it did not compare with either the Eifl or the Penmaenmawr quarries. At its height between 1900 and 1904 Gwylwyr employed over 100 men. During the same period Eifl had a workforce of 400 while the Penmaenmawr quarries employed over 1000 men between them. During the first decade of the 20th century there was still a considerable demand for granite setts, stimulated by the introduction of electrified street tramways in many large urban centres. This gave an additional boost to quarries like Gwylwyr.

The outbreak of the First World War virtually closed the Gwylwyr Quarry. In 1913-14 over 60 workers were still employed there. From 1916-1920 there was no production at all and subsequently setts began to give way to tar macadamised road surfaces. In the 1920's and 1930's the quarry remained open but the number of employees working there could be counted on one hand. In 1937 it provided work for just 2 quarrymen.

On Gwylwyr the tramway ran down a steep incline, crossed the Pistyll road at Wern (where the caravan site is now situated), then ran down to the shore and on to a wooden jetty extending into the sea, where ships were moored to be loaded with their cargoes. From August 1854 to November 1855 ten shiploads of setts were exported from Nefyn to Liverpool and Runcorn. It is possible to climb up to the quarry workings but, for those not willing or able to make that ascent, the greatly changed contours of the mountainside, the remains of the quarry buildings and the line of the tramway are all discernible from the lower end of the town. Furthermore, at low tide the stumps of the wooden pillars supporting the jetty at Wern can be seen sticking up out of the water. During World War II, when the threat of invasion loomed, this jetty was blown up.

Another local quarry was the one established by Herbert Thomas of Tŷ Mawr Farm on the foreshore at Penrhyn Bodeilias, the point at the north eastern end of the bay at Nefyn. It was known as the **Tŷ Mawr or Bodeilias Quarry**. In February 1861 this quarry was leased for 21 years to Richard Morris, a banker of Caernarfon, Hedworth Lee, a civil engineer of Caernarfon and William Arthur Darbishire, a slate proprietor. In November 1863, together with 4 other important shareholders from Lancashire, they formed the Tŷ Mawr Granite Company with a registered company office in High St, Bangor.

As already mentioned, in November 1864 the Tŷ Mawr Quarry was amalgamated with the Gwylwyr and Eifl quarries under the name of the Welsh Granite Co. Ltd., and Darbishire, Lee and Griffith of the old Tŷ Mawr Company became board members of the new company. The Tŷ Mawr Quarry was purchased for £1000 in cash and £5000 in shares. The plant, materials and stores at Tŷ Mawr were valued at £114 – 4s – 2d. In 1866 the former Tŷ Mawr directors left the board of the Welsh Granite Co. Ltd., and it was decided to sell off the Tŷ Mawr operation. In July 1876 the lease of the Tŷ Mawr Quarry was obtained by a Liverpool company trading as the Carnarvon Bay Granite Quarries, whose registered office was at 3 Brunswick St, Liverpool.

In 1878 the quarrying operation run by the Carnarvon Bay Company was sold to The Liverpool and Nefyn Granite Co. Ltd. with offices at 41 The Temple, Dale St, Liverpool. The purchase price was £2,400 in cash and £1800 in fully paid shares. The sale brochure indicates that there were 2 galleries, the lower one on the shore 15 feet above high water measuring 100 yds long and 50 feet high. There was a dock, a carpenter's shop, a smith's workshop and offices. The sale also included an anchor and chain, a weighing machine, buckets for loading vessels, a crane, 2 trolleys, 1 side tip wagon, 200 yds of rail with sleepers attached and the usual tools and sundries. This company was wound up in 1882.

By 1898 the Bodeilias Quarry was being worked by the Tŷ Mawr Granite Quarry Syndicate Co Ltd with offices at 11 Rumford Place, Liverpool. In November 1900 the Nefyn Bay Granite Co. Ltd. was formed to acquire the Bodeilias Quarry at Tŷ Mawr Farm. The directors were from Liverpool, Manchester and Middlewich and the head office was at 7 St James Square, Manchester. The terms of the lease were £20 per annum rent, merging into royalties of 3d per ton of setts, 6d per ton of stone blocks and 1d per ton of macadam. In 1901 84 workers were employed here but by 1907 the quarry had ceased to function and the company was dissolved in July 1908. This marked the end of commercial quarrying at Tŷ Mawr Farm. It is still possible to gain access to the Bodeilias galleries by walking along to the north eastern end of the beach at Nefyn, although no buildings remain.

The small quarry known as **Gwaith John Lloyd** can be seen on the side of the Mynydd behind Nefyn, in front of and below some whitewashed cottages. In January 1866 John Lloyd Jones of Llandwrog and James Hughes of Manchester took a 21 year lease from Lord Newborough on 73 acres on "Nefyn mountain" to quarry granite. The rent was £10 per annum with royalties of 2d per ton for paving stones and 1d per ton for macadamised stones. The 1868 Slater's Directory records that the quarry was being worked by "John Lloyd Jones and Co. of Nefyn" and the agent was R.S. Williams. For many years this quarry lay idle until in 1921-22 it was reopened by Henry Griffith of 37 High St, Blaenau Ffestiniog as the **Arvonia Quarry**. In 1925 Griffith was employing 32 men there. By 1931 the workforce had shrunk to 10 and in 1934 there were only 9 employees working either part time or on a seasonal basis. By 1937 production had ceased altogether at this quarry.

In June 1864 the Nefyn Granite Quarry Company was formed to work the **Moel Tŷ Gwyn Quarries**, known separately as the Vaenol Quarry and the Nanhoron Quarry, just inside the parish of Pistyll. The controlling shareholders and directors came from Manchester and Rochdale and the Company secretary was John Worthy Williams. The Vaenol Quarry was leased from the Vaenol Estate of Mr. Assheton Smith and the Nanhoron Quarry was leased from Mr. Francis W Lloyd Edwards of the Nanhoron Estate. A tramway was constructed down the side of Moel Tygwyn, and across the road in Pistyll to a sea wharf with sufficient depth for loading at all times of the tide.

In February 1879 these quarries were acquired by London merchants trading as the Nefyn Syenite Granite Company Ltd. with offices in Leadenhall St, London. The company also owned the 84 ton steamship *Edith* to transport the stone away. In 1881 the Moel Tŷ Gwyn Quarries were put up for sale by the Nefyn Syenite Granite Co. Ltd. and the sale included the quarries, the tramways and inclines, 2 stone-built offices, 2 weighing machine houses, a coal yard, 14 workmen's cottages, a corner shop, a coach house, stabling, a stone crusher, a steam engine as well as other items of plant and tools. At this time the Vaenol lease, dated 18th July 1878, was for 21 years at £50 per annum merging into a royalty of 3d. per ton for setts, 2d. per ton for metalling and 4d. per ton for dressed paving stones. The Nanhoron lease, dated 1st August, 1878, was for 40 years at a rent of £20 per annum for the first 20 years and £45 per annum for the remaining term with a royalty of two and a half pence per ton.

In 1881 another quarry was opened on top of Mynydd Nefyn adjacent to Carreg Lefain or Echo Mountain, as it is also called. This was the **Foel Dywyrch Quarry**. In 1886 the Nefyn United Granite Quarries (Carnarvonshire) Ltd. was formed to acquire the aforementioned Moel Tygwyn quarries and also to secure the Foel Dywyrch Quarry, which was leased from the Crown in January 1887 by its directors, Messrs Fox, Durrant and Jennings. The company offices were at 63 Queen Victoria St, London and another of its directors was R T Hermon Hodge MP. The company was finally dissolved in February 1903. Foel Dywyrch subsequently passed into the hands of the Nefyn Parish Council, which turned it into rough grazing land, the money raised in grazing charges being used for charitable purposes within the parish.

The **Carreg y Llam Quarry** is situated on the coast at Penrhyn Glas to the west of the village of Llithfaen. It was opened in 1911 by H J Wright who employed between 40 and 60 workers there from 1911-14. During the First World War the workforce dwindled and there were just 2 men working there in 1918. The fortunes of the quarry revived in 1920 when the London-based Carreg y Llam Quarries, with London offices at Marconi House in The Strand, took it over with H J Wright as one of its directors. The company built a new pier and from 1920 to 1937 between 45 and 70 men worked there, in addition to outworkers. The company also operated the steamships *Maggie Purves* and *Panmure*. In the late 1920's electrically driven stone crushers were installed for the production of macadam, railway ballast and aggregates. In 1950 Carreg y Llam Quarries sold out to the Amalgamated Roadstone Corporation Ltd, which had already acquired the neighbouring Porth y Nant Quarry. During the period between the two World Wars and the years immediately after World War II, several Nefyn men worked at the Carreg y Llam Quarry, for there was no longer such work to be found in the old Nefyn quarries.

During the second half of the 19th century a brickworks was established behind the beach at Morfa Nefyn and a wooden jetty was constructed jutting out into the sea. For many years its tall chimney stack dominated the Morfa skyline, providing a useful landmark from both land and sea. The Morfa brickworks closed before the First World War, and today its site is a National Trust car park.

Granite is no longer quarried along the northern coast of Llŷn, although, as has been noted, ample evidence of this industrial activity still remains in the form of abandoned quarry workings. The extraction of granite in Caernarfonshire cannot be considered a major industry when compared with the scale of slate quarrying within the county. Futhermore, the Llŷn granite quarries cannot be compared in importance with those of the Penmaenmawr region. Nevertheless, it must be recognised that the quarries in and around Nefyn provided valuable employment opportunities within the area and their contribution to the region's economy for over 120 years ought not to be discounted.

18. CHURCH AND CHAPEL

The great religious upheavals which occurred under successive monarchs during the 16th century appear to have had little impact in places like Nefyn which was so remote from the seat of power. The majority of parishioners were illiterate and many parish clergy at that time were not highly educated. It is probable that they would not have understood or been particularly interested in the great doctrinal issues and matters of conviction which arose as a result of the Protestant Reformation and the establishment of the Anglican Church. What mattered most of all to the ordinary folk was the routine of attendance at services of worship – the weekly Sunday devotions, the acts of worship to celebrate the Christian festivals and the services to mark important family occasions such as baptisms, marriages and burials. Despite the profound changes which had occurred, many of the old traditional practices in worship continued in many Welsh churches, particularly in the remoter areas.

Since the mid 17th century groups of fervent Independents, based in Pwllheli and in the parishes of Llangybi and Llangian, had been active in Llŷn. Yet by 1800 there had not been a significant increase in Nonconformist numbers in these parts. In the town of Nefyn at that time there were modest congregations of Calvinistic Methodists and Baptists meeting in small purpose-built chapels, while a small Independent congregation was meeting regularly for Sunday worship in a private house. At the turn of the century the Anglican Church still 'reigned' supreme.

By 1836 the pattern of religious adherence was very different. The first 3 decades of the 19th century saw an explosion of Nonconformist membership more dramatic than anything the area had seen before. The number of separate Nonconformist congregations in Nefyn, each with its own building for worship, had doubled to 4 since there were now Calvinistic, Baptist, Independent and Wesleyan chapels. Growth among the Calvinistic Methodists had been particularly rapid, for their membership had quickly trebled in Llŷn. The Anglican Church was unable to stem this Nonconformist tide, despite an extensive programme of church restoration and rebuilding. Funded by the principal landowners in Nefyn, the parish church of St Mary was rebuilt in 1827 on the site formerly occupied by previous ancient churches. The new building had a seating capacity of 250, but in 1836 the curate wrote complainingly that his "average congregation hardly numbers 30 because 99 out of every 100 are Dissenters"[1].

Over the next 15 years the Dissenting chapels continued to prosper.

The 1851 Religious Census recorded that Nefyn parish church had just 14% of the available seating for worship, while the Nonconformist chapels in the town had 86%. In terms of attendance at Sunday worship, a total of just over 90 worshippers attended the two Anglican Sunday services, while Nonconformist attendances totalled over 1900 each week. Even if one allows for a slight manipulation of the figures presented to the Census, it is clear that the swing to Nonconformity had been overwhelming and decisive. In the space of 50 years there had been a transformation in the pattern of religious adherence in Nefyn and this change was reflected throughout Caernarfonshire generally.

There followed a series of religious revivals, characterised by renewed zeal and a great evangelising spirit, such as the huge revival of 1859 and the last great revival of 1905. Hearty Welsh hymn singing and rousing preaching played an important part in chapel services. During the second half of the 19th century and the early years of the 20th century, Nonconformist congregations continued to dominate, and the chapel ministers and elders were forced to build ever larger buildings to accommodate their increasing numbers.

The **Calvinistic Methodists** were the first Dissenting group to form a congregation in Nefyn, following the visits to the area in 1741 by Howell Harris, a Breconshire schoolmaster and evangelist and by Daniel Rowland, a Cardiganshire curate in 1747. At that time, despite considerable opposition in Nefyn to these visits, the seeds were sown and a small group of Calvinists began to hold services in the thatched cottage of John Parry, tailor, and later in the house of John William Humphrey at Cae Rhug, where it is said he eventually built a small annexe on to the end of his dwelling for use as a chapel. The first purpose-built Nefyn Calvinistic chapel was built in 1785. As the congregation increased, additional accommodation was provided either by rebuilding or enlarging the existing chapel in 1805, 1826, 1833 and 1875. The 1875 building was a large imposing structure, capable of seating over 1000 people. In 1884 an organ was purchased and installed, contrary to the wishes of some members of the congregation. At its inauguration 3 of the elders protested by sitting silently in their pews during the singing, while another sat tight-lipped and facing the wall with his back to the organ. In 1905 a sasiwn (a Calvinistic Association gathering for the area) was held at Nefyn and 1300 people packed into the chapel for the service.

In 1776 a group of **Baptist** missionaries from South Wales toured Llŷn, preaching at Nefyn probably in August 1777. Subsequently, a small group of Baptists began to meet regularly for worship at a house in Penpalment, and services were held here until the first Baptist chapel was built on the

Fron in 1785. Owing to the energetic and determined evangelism of Rev Christmas Evans and subsequently other Baptist ministers and members of the congregation, attendances increased and a new large square chapel was built on the same site in 1850. Before the middle of the 19th century the Baptists in Nefyn had split into 2 separate congregations – the main congregation of Baptists who continued to meet at Capel y Fron and the Particular Baptists who met at the Club House belonging to Clwb Mawr in Y Maes. In 1904 a much larger Baptist chapel building, Capel Seion, was built at the bottom of Stryd y Plas to meet the needs of the growing congregation. The site of the old Baptist chapels can be reached by walking down Stryd y Plas and bearing right at the house called Tan y dderwen. The graveyard of the old Baptist chapels is to be found up the steep hill on the right hand side.

By the late 18th century the **Independents** or Congregationalists were holding services at Wern Beuda Glas, Mrs Roberts's old house at Wern. In the early years of the 19th century worship was transferred to the home of Griffith Williams, carpenter, on the Fron, where services were held until the first Congregational chapel was built on land leased from Richard Edwards of Nanhoron in February 1827. During the 1870's many Independent quarry workers came to Nefyn from Penmaenmawr and therefore in 1880 it was decided to build the present chapel building, Capel Soar at Pen y Bryn, so that the growing congregation could be more readily accommodated.

The **Wesleyan** movement came to Nefyn at the start of the 19th century, when 3 Wesleyan evangelists visited the town during their Caernarfonshire mission. In 1804 the first small Wesleyan chapel was built where the Madryn Hall was later built. In 1881 this chapel was replaced by the present larger building, Capel Moreia in Stryd Moreia, and the old chapel was demolished to make way for the Madryn Hall.

At the time of the 1851 Religious Census there was no church or chapel building in Morfa village. For many years the inhabitants living in this part of the parish had been forced to walk each Sunday to the places of worship in the town until they began to gather for worship in houses and cottages. Eventually it was decided to build purpose-built chapels in the centre of the village.

The folk of Morfa, too, were split along denominational lines. The Baptist chapel (Caersalem) was the first one to be completed in 1853 with seating for 160. It still stands opposite Morfa Nefyn Post Office. About a year later the Methodists, the predominant Nonconformist group in Morfa Nefyn, built a substantial square chapel on the opposite side of the road. Their congregation grew steadily until by 1880 the original chapel building was considered too small. Therefore in 1882 a larger and much more imposing building (Moriah) was opened with a seating capacity of 500. In 1862 the Morfa Congregationalists also built a chapel (Tabernacl), and in 1871 St Mary's Church at Morfa was opened for members of the Church in Wales. It had the powerful support of the local gentry, especially Richard Lloyd Edwards of Nanhoron who donated the land on which the church was built. Just over 30 years later in 1904 the Church in Wales built the new parish church of St David at Pen y Bryn on the Morfa Road. In Nefyn parish, as in Wales generally, the closing decades of the 19th century and the beginning of the 20th century were characterised by an intense religious zeal and wholesale attendance at Sunday worship.

A notable local character in the period between the two world wars was Tom Williams, who was brought up on a small farm facing the sea at Bodeilias on the slopes of Mynydd Gwylwyr. He had worked as a quarryman and when war broke out in 1914 he joined the army. It was while he was serving in the trenches on the Western Front and at Gallipoli that he vowed to spend the rest of his life preaching the gospel. After the war, although suffering serious wounds from which he never fully recuperated, he trained for the ministry in Aberystwyth and became a minister in South Wales. Following a disagreement with the chapel authorities there, he returned to the Nefyn area where he became an itinerant evangelist. He was a familiar sight preaching and leading hymn singing in the open air on Y Groes, on the beach and on the cliff top. He achieved a reputation as a fine preacher and crowds flocked to hear him deliver his word. Throughout North Wales he became famous as 'Twm Nefyn', and a memorial plaque incorporating his relief portrait can be seen on the front wall of Capel Bethania in Pistyll.

The religious fervour of the 1905 revival and the enthusiasm generated by the charismatic preaching of Twm Nefyn during the 1920's did not prevent a steady decline in chapel and church going during the second half of the 20th century. The huge Nefyn Calvinistic Chapel in Stryd y Ffynnon was demolished to be replaced by a small modern building much more in keeping with the size of its congregation, while the large Baptist Capel Seion, which was once filled with worshippers, has now closed for lack of people to keep it going, the last service being held there at Easter 2001. In Morfa the Congregational Chapel closed in the 1960's, and Caersalem Baptist chapel closed its doors for the last time towards the end of 2003. The places of worship which remain open within the parish no longer attract the large congregations of the glory days at the end of the 19th century.

The periods of great religious revival, tremendous spiritual fervour and enormous Nonconformist congregations during times past are in sharp contrast to the situation today. It is astonishing to think that in 1851 the combined average weekly attendance at Sunday services in Nefyn was recorded as 2347; but equally staggering has been the fall off in attendance at worship during the past 70 years or so, a secularisation of society which has been repeated right across the country.

The growth of Welsh Nonconformity during the 19th and early 20th centuries was not only impressive but it was also historically significant, for the population of Wales became divided along Church and Chapel lines. The emergent Nonconformist middle classes (the shipowners, master mariners and artisans) supported the Whigs politically in opposition to the Anglican Tory landowners and quarry owners, and it was the middle classes who assumed the lead in local affairs. They not only became leaders within their chapels but they also took on leadership roles within their communities; for example they were instrumental in the establishment of undenominational and Board schools. Furthermore, the Nonconformist chapels did a great deal to preserve Welsh as a dynamic language, and it was the preachings of Nonconformity and a succession of religious revivals which led to the abandonment of many old Welsh social customs, no longer considered acceptable in a Christian society. Therefore the rise of Welsh Nonconformity not only brought about a revolution in the pattern of religious attendance but it also helped to bring about a transformation in Welsh society itself.

(1) The Report on the Borough of Nefyn, 1836.

19. SCHOOLS

During the 18th and early 19th centuries in Nefyn, education was in the hands of 3 private adventure schools and the Circulating Schools of Griffith Jones. Private schools at this time were usually run by untrained and often barely literate masters and mistresses, while the vast majority of ordinary Nefyn folk could not afford the money that was required for attendance.

The Circulating Schools movement of Griffith Jones, a Carmarthenshire rector, was founded to teach people to read the Bible in Welsh, a commendable effort to reduce the high level of illiteracy among the great mass of the ordinary people. Griffiths used itinerant teachers to tour the Welsh parishes, setting up each school for a period of about 3 months at a time, usually in the parish church during the winter months when local farms were less busy. During the second half of the 18th century 12 such school sessions were held in Nefyn, providing instruction for a total of 756 children and adults. Griffith Jones died in 1761 and his movement ceased to function after about 1771.

The vacuum left by the collapse of the Circulating Schools was subsequently filled by the Sunday School movement, which also instructed children and adults in the scriptures. It was initiated in North Wales by the Calvinistic Methodists under the direction of Thomas Charles of Bala, and the idea was soon adopted by other denominations. By 1836 there were several Sunday Schools in the parish run by Nonconformists. They were held in the local Nefyn chapels and in people's homes in Morfa village. However there was still no National School in the town and parish, although the curate of Boduan and Nefyn had tried to raise funds for the maintenance of a master. Therefore, at this time, most Nefyn children were denied any form of regular schooling.

In about 1840 a plot of land was purchased by the Church authorities at Penbryn Holborn and a National School was built. But from the start the school was plagued by financial problems. In 1843 the vicar of Nefyn wrote to Lady Newborough requesting her £2 subscription towards the school. In his letter he explained that the master, who had 80 children in his care, had only received £26 during the previous year, for the parents were £20 in arrears. In 1847 the total amount of money subscribed was just £5 and the 3 main landowners in Nefyn all declined to contribute. Furthermore, by this time the majority of Nefyn folk were Nonconformists, many of whom did not wish their children to learn the Church catechism or to attend Church service each Sunday, since both were prerequisites for school attendance. Consequently, many Nefyn residents refused to send their children to the National School, continuing to rely on the Nonconformist Sunday Schools for instruction. The more affluent ship owners, master mariners and artisans preferred to send their children to the local private schools.

In about 1850 a group of leading Nonconformists made moves to establish an undenominational British School in Nefyn, along the lines of the British and Foreign Schools' Society. They invited the Society's agent in North Wales to Nefyn, and following a meeting with him, they formed a committee to establish a British School in the club room at Y Maes. Soon local subscriptions enabled the present school building on the Morfa Road to be built, and the British School moved into its new building in 1859. Nefyn could now boast a National School run by the Church authorities, an undenominational British School and several small private schools.

During the 19th century several navigational classes were established in Nefyn to teach young seamen the rudiments of navigation. David Wilson, a customs officer at Porth Dinllaen, John Thomas, local cobbler and notable mathematician, and subsequently, Hugh Davies, a nailer living in Stryd y Llan, all taught navigational skills to ambitious young Nefyn seamen. Another navigation school was established in Morfa Nefyn at 'Ysgol Sion Peters'.

In 1870 Forster's Education Act sought to establish a universal state education system by setting up local School Boards which would establish Board schools. The Boards consisted of elected members with the power to levy a local rate to finance their school and enforce attendance. This system was designed to fill the gaps left by the voluntary societies and would ensure a school place for every 5-13 year old within reasonable walking distance.

The people of Nefyn were opposed to the establishment of a School Board, for at a poll of ratepayers in 1871, the notion was firmly rejected by 145 votes to 51. Church people were opposed because they wished to protect the interests of their National School, and the majority of ratepayers were reluctant to incur additional compulsory charges on the town's rates. However, a small group of influential Nonconformist local leaders saw the advantages of a Board School. By 1874 Nefyn ratepayers were still refusing to voluntarily establish a School Board, and so in November 1874, under Section 10 of the Act, a School Board was compulsorily established by law. The British School was forced to disband and its building was used to house the newly established Board School. The establishment of the Board School also sounded the death knell of the National School, which still had to rely on voluntary contributions, and in

1881 the National School closed.

Private schools still continued to operate in Nefyn during the second half of the 19th century. Slater's Directory of 1858 recorded 3 private schools belonging to Richard Jones, James Roberts and John Roberts. 10 years later, Slater's 1868 Directory mentioned Miss Jones Infants' school at Nefyn and Jane Linton's girls' school at Porth Dinllaen, which some Nefyn girls attended. An interesting Directory advertisement of 1886 provides details of Mrs. Hugh Jones's "Ladies Select School" at Plas Tirion, Morfa Nefyn, which took boarders and day pupils and which offered instruction in languages, music, drawing and needlework.[1] By the early 1900's Plas Tirion was in the hands of Laurence Hart and his wife who ran 'Morfa Nefyn College for Girls' on the premises. This was a boarding school for young ladies who were afforded a Christian education with the emphasis upon discipline, manners and deportment. The headmistress was Miss Mary Thomas B.A. who also provided a variety of outdoor pursuits. The school at Plas Tirion closed in 1907 following the death of the owner.

Today the only schools within the parish of Nefyn are the 2 primary schools. Ysgol Nefyn is housed in the former British School/Board School building to which additional accommodation has been added. Ysgol Morfa was established for the children of Morfa Nefyn in 1908, when it was accommodated in a temporary wood and corrugated iron structure, which was not replaced by a new purpose-built brick building until 1981. The remains of the old Nefyn National School can still be seen incorporated into a dwelling called Penbryn Holborn, which is situated on the road leading towards Y Bryncynan.

(1) Porter's Postal Directory 1886.

20. COMMUNICATIONS, TRANSPORT, WATER AND FUEL

In the 18th and early 19th centuries Llŷn is frequently portrayed as an isolated, remote, backward region at the western extremity of northern Wales, completely cut off from the rest of the world. But this impression is surely a little misleading as far as Nefyn is concerned. Whilst it is true that the internal lines of communication were very poor, there was plenty of contact with the outside world in a seafaring community like Nefyn where it was usual for people to travel by sea to other coastal places in Wales and England. New ideas were brought in by mariners sailing to other parts, and by drovers taking cattle to the English Midlands and to London. Many of the local gentry were much travelled outside Wales, and it was the gentry and the well-established seafaring families who were first to assume family surnames.

If Llŷn was not a totally isolated and stagnant backwater, it must have appeared so to travellers like Pennant, who travelled over land through Nefyn in the second half of the 18th century. Until the early 19th century most Llŷn roads were little better than dirt trackways, first established through common usage by traders and travellers before and during the medieval period. They were unsurfaced, unfenced and undrained tracks across fields and commons, connecting village with village. Road repair was the responsibility of the parish but all too frequently this task was neglected. Consequently, these routes were often in such a poor state that they were virtually impassable. Most travel locally was on foot, by donkey or on the small but sturdy Welsh cob. Writing in 1595 a writer described the county of Caernarfon as the "most rugged, unpassable, barren country in Wales"[1].

The earliest available map of Nefyn, dating from 1775 reveals that, by this time, the basic pattern of the main routes in and out of the town was already well established. There was the road north-eastwards through Pistyll towards Caernarfon and the route westwards to Edern and Tudweiliog, and then down the peninsula, following the northern coast. This was the ancient medieval pilgrim way to Ynys Enlli and the principal route through the town. The road to the southeast led to Ceidio and Madryn while the route eastwards over the mountain linked Nefyn with Boduan and Llannor and ultimately to Pwllheli. All four routes converged in the middle of Nefyn at a crossroads called Y Groes.

At this time the dwellings were concentrated mainly in two areas - at the top end of the town (around Y Maes, Y Groes and Stryd y Plas) and at the lower end in Penisa'r dre around the church and the water mill. The haphazard arrangement of the roads in Nefyn, an organic Welsh settlement, is in marked contrast to planted 'Edwardian' towns like Caernarfon and Conwy, with their regular street plans. Entries in the Nefyn Court Book 1756-82 record that the Grand Jury opened 2 new roads within the borough, one on 26th May 1764 and the other on 24th May 1777.

Donkeys wearing panniers were probably one of the earliest means of transporting goods in and around Nefyn, for they were best suited to negotiating the difficult road conditions. There were still several Nefyn donkey drivers operating from Nefyn when coaches and wagons were being used. Moses Jones of Stryd y Llan carried goods to Pwllheli using donkeys. John Hughes, of Tanybragdy and later Tuhwntirafon, operated a business carrying farm produce and goods to Pwllheli, using donkeys and a cart. Asaph Jones used a donkey and cart to sell herrings round the peninsula, while Richard Williams of Morfa Nefyn ran a donkey and cart between Morfa and Pwllheli. Thomas W Davies of Penybryn sold herrings and greengrocery all over Llŷn, transporting his produce in a cart pulled by a donkey.

In 1809-11 Hyde-Hall wrote of the roads in Nefyn, "In addition to the county road which passes through the parish from Pistyll to Edern, the new turnpike road traverses the southern part of it for a short distance on its way to Porthynllaen"[2]. It was the Turnpike Trusts, established to build and maintain new toll roads, which brought about improvements in travel during the late 18th and early 19th centuries. As early as 1770 proposals were put forward for a turnpike road from Llangynog in Montgomeryshire, through Bala, over Traeth Mawr and across the peninsula to Porth Dinllaen to provide a shorter route to Ireland.

The Porth Dinllaen Turnpike Trust had to wait until 1803 before it was finally established by Act of Parliament. The Trust built the first section of road from Porth Dinllaen to Tan y Graig, Boduan. From here the turnpike was constructed almost in a straight line across the peninsula passing through Y Ffôr and Chwilog to a point near Llanystumdwy. Here it met another leg of the turnpike which went from Tan y Graig through Pwllheli and then along the coast to Llanystumdwy. From this point where the two roads met, the turnpike proceeded via Cricieth, Tremadoc, Aberglaslyn and Beddgelert to Capel Curig, where it linked up with the Capel Curig Trust turnpike. The reclamation of Traeth Mawr begun at about roughly the same time by Madocks, and his building of the embankment and road across it, opened up Llŷn by road to Merionethshire. The turnpikes made Caernarfonshire more accessible by land and provided a great stimulus to the economic development of the county generally.

As roads began to improve Nefyn carriers using horses and wagons began to provide a service carrying goods around Llŷn. In the 1840's George Hughes carried goods regularly between Caernarfon and Nefyn. Robert Williams, Bryn Bach, and his 2 sons, Evan and William, were listed as carriers on the 1871 Census. Griffith Jones is recorded as a carrier on the 1881 Census.

However, in the mid 19th century some local roads were still in a calamitous state. For example, in 1847 the aforementioned Nefyn carrier, George Hughes, complained bitterly about the poor condition of the road between Llanaelhaearn and Nefyn. He journeyed regularly between Nefyn and Caernarfon, and he wrote that the route over the mountains past Yr Eifl was so bad that he had lost 8 horses on this stretch of road in 6 years, the last of his horses suddenly dropping dead in the harness.

As roads improved still further other enterprising local individuals began to use horse-drawn coaches to operate regular passenger services between Nefyn and local destinations. A famous Nefyn coachman was Richard Davies, who took over the Nanhoron Arms in Stryd y Ffynnon from where he ran a regular service between Nefyn and Pwllheli. Griffith Jones of Castle Inn, Morfa Nefyn, was a driver for Richard Davies, before starting up on his own with a 4 in hand and a 3 in hand, which he drove from Edern to Pwllheli 6 days a week. At the same time David Davies of the Madryn Arms, Nefyn, ran a small 4 wheeled coach, carrying people and goods from Nefyn to Pwllheli. Sometimes he collected goods from the ships which came to Porth Dinllaen, carrying them to distant parts of the peninsula. William Jones of Cae'r Pwll, Morfa Nefyn, drove a coach and 4 in hand from Edern to Pwllheli, while John Elias, Penpalment, ran a very successful coaching business. He started with 2 horses and a wagonette which ran between Nefyn and Pwllheli. Later he drove a 4 wheeled coach with 3 in hand, carrying about 16 people. The service ran from Edern to Pwllheli via Morfa Nefyn and Nefyn, and it continued to operate until the motor omnibuses started running. John Elias also drove his coach from Nefyn to Caernarfon. His horses were stabled at Penpalment where the Spar Supermarket now stands. These regular coach services were the means by which sailors returning on their ships to Caernarfon or Pwllheli were able to get home to Nefyn.

When Captain Henry Parry retired from going to sea he took over the Nanhoron Arms and the coaching business from Richard Davies. He was succeeded by his son, Owen Parry, who imported horses from Ireland, broke them in and then sold them to coach drivers throughout the peninsula. He employed a coachman called Robert Roberts of Tŷ Popty which stood next door to where the fire station is now situated at the bottom of Stryd y Ffynnon in Penisa'r dre. Later Robert Roberts set up in business on his own with a coach house next to his cottage.

Before the coming of the railways, horse-drawn coaches carried the mail from Caernarfon to Llŷn as well as providing regular passenger services between Nefyn and other places on the peninsula. Daniel Parry, Tŷ Cerrig, drove the Mail Coach from Caernarfon to Pwllheli for about 9 years, after which he started his own coaching business. Letters were taken from Pwllheli around the peninsula by a donkey and gig, which at one time was driven by John Owen Jones of Tan y Maes.

During the first decade of the 20th century the age of motor transport came to Nefyn, and Cambrian Railways started to run a pair of 2 cylinder 16 hp motor omnibuses between Pwllheli railway station, Nefyn, Morfa Nefyn and Edern. Each omnibus had 2 doors and seating for 22 passengers. Two passengers sat next to the driver, 8 sat in the forward compartment and there was room for 12 in the rear compartment. Very shortly afterwards a Morfa coaching firm bought a motor omnibus and began to run a motor bus service from Morfa to Pwllheli several times a week. About the same time Owen Parry of Nefyn abandoned his horse-drawn coaches and founded another local omnibus company called the Nefyn and District Omnibus Company which also ran a service to Pwllheli. Its depot was situated a few yards beyond Shop Zebra at the end of Stryd y Felin. The buses, which were square solid-looking vehicles constructed of wood upon a metal chassis, were built by John Parry in his workshop at Glandon, just outside the town on the road to Pistyll. Immediately before the outbreak of the First World War the Morfa bus company and Owen Parry's Nefyn and District Omnibus Company combined to compete with the Cambrian Company.

Soon after the First World War ended, Garwen Hughes, a Nefyn hairdresser, started a rival Nefyn company called the Blue Bus Company with its depot in Stryd y Llan. This garage can still be seen although it is no longer used for that purpose. As J Ifor Davies reminisces, there was considerable competition for passengers as well as for fast journey times between the drivers of the two rival Nefyn companies. In the decade leading up to the outbreak of the Second World the railway bus company and both Nefyn 'bus firms were absorbed into the Crossville Company which continued to run local bus services until the 1990's. Today, once again, it is a local Nefyn-based 'bus firm, Nefyn Coaches with its depot on the Morfa Road, which runs the local 'bus services.

In the 1890's Abergeirch Bay to the west of Porth Dinllaen was selected for the North Wales terminus of a very different and technologically

121

advanced form of communication – the telegraph to Ireland. Cables were laid under the Irish Sea and a small building was constructed in the bay to house the machinery necessary for the operation of the system. The remains of this building can still be seen, and when the tide is out it is possible to catch sight of the remnants of the cable.

Until the early years of the 20th century the folk of Nefyn had relied upon wells and springs for their water supply, and the carrying of buckets of water from the town's well was one of the daily chores for local inhabitants. Dwellings on the mountain had their own wells and springs but the well at the top of Stryd y Ffynnon was the main source of water for the town. For several years polluted water had caused outbreaks of typhoid and cholera in many urban centres. Alarmed by this, towns such as Bangor, Caernarfon, Porthmadog, Pwllheli and Cricieth had all built their own reservoirs between 1854 and 1883. In 1905-6 a small reservoir was constructed for Nefyn on the slopes of the Mynydd, and water was piped down from here into the town. The reservoir was opened by Rt. Hon. David Lloyd George and the occasion was marked by a procession of all the local schoolchildren headed by the Nefyn town band, followed by a water display on Y Groes by firemen from Pwllheli.

For centuries, Nefyn folk had relied upon open cottage fires for heating their homes and for cooking. Leland, after travelling through the Nefyn area sometime between 1536 and 1539, wrote, "They burne turffs, ferne and gorses otherwise called fyrres"[3]. Such types of fuel continued to be used by the majority of Nefyn folk until well into the nineteenth century. After the tax on coal brought in by sea had been abolished in 1831, more people were better able to afford culm and coal shipped in mainly from the coalfields of South Wales, the Dee Estuary and from Liverpool. During the dark winter evenings homes were lit by rushlights or home-made tallow candles, and later on oil lamps and wax candles were used. An electricity supply did not arrive in Nefyn until about 1928, when it was brought to both the town and Morfa village from the quarry at Carreg y Llam, where it was used to operate the crushers which processed the lumps of granite into crushed stone. It is amazing to think that there are people living in Nefyn today who can still remember what life was like in the days before the town had an electricity supply. It is even more surprising to realize that the daily routine of fetching water from the town's well is only just beyond living memory for one or two local inhabitants.

(1) Cited by Dodd, A.H. in *A History of Caernarvonshire*
(2) Hyde-Hall, E. *A Description of Caernarvonshire, 1809-11.*
(3) *Leland's Itinerary in Wales, 1536-9* ed. Lucy Toulmin Smith.

21. THE RELIEF OF THE NEFYN POOR

The Elizabethan Poor Law Acts had sought to deal with the increasing problem of poverty and vagrancy by providing machinery for poor relief in every parish. These acts delegated relief of the poor to Overseers of the Poor, who were responsible to the parish vestry and the Justices of the Peace. Overseers had the power to raise revenue for poor relief from the local rates and this source was usually supplemented by monies from alms giving.

In Caernarfonshire poor rates do not seem to have been collected until the second half of the 18th century. At that time extreme cases of poverty were relieved from other sources, such as Church alms collections, bequests from the wills of wealthy persons and the generosity of the local gentry. In Nefyn during the early 18th century it was recorded that, when the herring harvest had failed and when food was scarce and expensive, the poor fishermen of Nefyn were given corn by John Owen of Plasyngheidio. "They did not have anything with which to pay for corn; they paid if they were able when God filled their nets again"[1]. Bequests to the poor of Nefyn were made in the wills of wealthy expatriate Welshmen like Roderick Lloyd of Lincolns Inn, Middx. (1728/9) and Sir William Wynne of Mary Le Bone, Middx. (1754).

Poor relief in Nefyn was also provided out of the fines imposed at the Nefyn Court. Hugh Griffith (Nov 1756) had to pay 1s 6d to the poor, while Margaret Arthur was ordered to give 2s 0d for poor relief. Jane Williams, spinster (Oct 1759) and Ann Joseph (Feb 1762) both had to donate 12 one penny loaves to the poor. Catherine Hughes (Aug 1763) and Robert Jones (July 1766) were required to contribute 1s 0d and 2s 6d respectively.

By the outbreak of the American War of Independence in 1776, parish poor rates were being levied in most Caernarfonshire parishes, but it was during the Napoleonic Wars that the greatest hardship was caused to Nefyn folk. The price of corn soared and the catastrophic rise in the tax on salt hit the herring fishers of Nefyn particularly hard. Subsequently, the enclosure of the commons around Nefyn deprived the ordinary townsfolk of their traditional right to graze animals and cut turfs for fuel. Some squatters, who had established themselves on encroachments at the margins of the commons and who could not provide legal proof of ownership, lost their homes with only scant financial compensation. Furthermore, the heavy tax on coal shipped in by sea was still in place (it was not lifted until 1831) and therefore obtaining fuel for warmth and cooking became a crippling burden, especially for the poorest members of the community.

The population of Nefyn had risen greatly during the first 3 decades of the 19th century, from 1028 in 1801 to 1,726 in 1831. From 1793 to 1803, after 10 years of war, the Poor Rate in Caernarfonshire as a whole had risen from just over £400 to £9,000. By 1819 the poor rate for the entire county had rocketed to £20,000. Writing of Nefyn during the Napoleonic Wars, Hyde-Hall stated, "The poor rate is described as greatly increased"[2]. The Overseers were finding it difficult to cope. In 1803 the total money raised for Nefyn poor relief was £95 .1s .8d, but the amount expended on the poor was £146 . 19s . 8d. During that year 31 adults and 20 children were given relief, while a further 17 people were granted occasional assistance.

The Act of Settlement 1662 had guaranteed the right of a person to receive poor relief from the parish only if that person had been born in the parish, had rented property in the parish, had paid a poor rate there, had been apprenticed in the parish for 7 years or more or had lived in that parish for at least 10 years. According to the Act any pauper who could not prove right of settlement according to any of the above criteria, would be denied relief and would be forcibly removed from that parish to the place of his or her birth.

The ever increasing burden of the Poor Rate caused parishes to squabble more and more over the removal and settlement of paupers. Cases were passed to the Quarter Sessions and it was the magistrates who had to make the necessary rulings. In Sept and Oct 1801 the parish of Nefyn was appealing against the removal of Robert David, labourer, from the parish of Abererch to Nefyn and the matter was referred to the next Quarter Sessions at Caernarfon. At the Hilary Quarter Session 1819 an order was made for the removal, from the parish of Llanbeblig to Nefyn, of two pauper children, William and Catherine Hughes, who had been deserted by their father.

By 1836 the Poor Rate assessment in Nefyn had risen to £322 which was described in the Nefyn Report of that year as being "very heavy". Nearly half of the relief money was used to pay the rents of paupers' cottages, for the Overseers were renting a number of dwellings within the town and on the mountain from local landowners, like Lord Newborough and the Edwards family of Nanhoron. Financial relief was given to able-bodied men who could not find employment and it was stated in 1836, "We do not set them to work because we have nothing for them to do". It was further emphasised, "There are indeed many poor people here", and this state of affairs was attributed especially to the effects of enclosure and the failure of the herring harvest for 6 or 7 years. The writer added, "We have no poor-house (workhouse) where the able-bodied could be set to work"[3]. Although there was great alarm and agitation at the ever increasing poor rate levy, Caernarfonshire parishes suffered a smaller poor rate rise than the more industrialised parishes of North Wales. Furthermore, Caernarfonshire as a whole levied a lower amount per head of population than any other North Wales county.

It was the enormous rise in the poor rates generally in Britain which prompted the Whig government of the time to appoint a commission to look into the provision for the Britain's poor, and this resulted in the Poor Law Amendment Act of 1834. This act introduced a new system of relief involving unions of parishes, each run by a Board of Guardians. The central idea was that outdoor relief should be abolished in favour of relief given within a Union workhouse built specifically for that purpose.

Under the Act Nefyn fell within the Pwllheli Union, which served all the parishes of Llŷn, as well as 5 in Eifionydd and 1 in Arfon. This amounted to a total of 32 parishes, where the people were predominantly engaged in agriculture, fishing and maritime activity. This new Act was passed just prior to another substantial increase in pauperism, owing to the economic recession of the 1840's, when the poorest members of society were forced to live mainly on barley bread and potatoes. Butter, cheese and meat were luxuries that many poor labourers and widows could not afford. The situation was even worse during the winter months when employment were scarce. It has been estimated that about one tenth of the population of Llŷn were paupers during the middle years of the 19th century and that many others were on the fringes of poverty. In places like Nefyn relative affluence and abject poverty existed side by side.

Wealthy local landowners continued to donate money for the relief of the poor. A letter of thanks written in 1844 by Rev Jones of Nefyn to Sir Robert Williams Vaughan expresses gratitude for Sir Robert's £15 contribution to the Nefyn poor. Sometimes Nefyn residents, who had fallen on hard times, were driven to asking for financial help from wealthy local landlords. In 1839 Elizabeth Parry wrote to Lord Newborough requesting a donation, as she had just lost her husband, the driver of a coach between Nefyn and Pwllheli, and she could not afford to provide for her 6 children. George Hughes, carrier, was forced to request charity from Lord Newborough in order to provide for his 6 children when his haulage business ran into difficulties.

The Pwllheli Guardians were one of the first boards in Caernarfonshire to build a workhouse in compliance with the 1834 Act. It was opened in 1840 in Ala Road, Pwllheli, and it had accommodation for 200 inmates. Although the Pwllheli Union had built this workhouse, and despite the fact that there was a great deal of poverty within the area covered by the

Union, relatively few paupers were committed to it during the 1850's. Instead, substantial numbers of the district's poor were still receiving outdoor relief. The 1851 Census reveals that, in Nefyn, there were 70 paupers living within the parish, 3 males and 67 females, mostly widows and spinsters. At that time only 2 Nefyn folk were resident within the workhouse, and they were Robert Jones, a 68 year old former sailor and John Thomas, a 48 year old shoemaker. In May 1860 the number of 'outdoor' paupers relieved by the Pwllheli Union was 2251 but the Ala Road workhouse contained only 36 inmates. In the 61 years from 1853 to 1914 only 25 Nefyn-born folk died within the workhouse and this figure included 6 infants under 12 months old.

Fear of the workhouse among ordinary folk was considerable, because conditions there were described as very harsh, austere and even squalid. The Pwllheli Board of Guardians adopted a policy of deterrence in an attempt to keep the poor rate down to an acceptable level. Food was adequate but uninspiring, for it consisted of oatmeal, buttermilk, potatoes, bread, herrings plus a little meat, cheese and lobscouse. Living conditions were depressing and the workhouse building was forbidding. Although the sexes were segregated, there was no attempt to classify inmates, so that paupers of all ages and conditions (including the mentally deranged) were accommodated together. The inmates slept on boards without any mattress and they ate their food using their fingers. The able-bodied at Ala Road were required to undertake tedious work such as picking oakum, sorting junk, chopping wood, carrying water and scrubbing and cleaning. There was a workhouse school but the education it provided was inadequate, for a report of 1847-8 condemned its provision. Although the central authorities (The Poor Law Commissioners in London) struggled to improve the lot of workhouse paupers, the Pwllheli Guardians were reluctant to upgrade the standards at Ala Road because of the cost implications. Some dietary improvements were introduced but as late as 1900 Ala Road Workhouse was criticised in an inspector's report because hot water was not provided for baths, only seaweed was provided for bedding and no cutlery was provided at mealtimes.

By 1921 the Pwllheli workhouse was more akin to a poorly-staffed geriatric hospital. At that time there were 50 inmates, 21 males and 29 females, of whom only one of each sex was able bodied. The remainder were invalids, who, for the most part, were confined to their beds, and yet they were looked after by a staff of just 4, none of whom was a trained nurse. Because of inadequate staffing and despite the best efforts of those in charge of the inmates, an article dated 27th August 1921 highlighted the neglect of these old, poor and vulnerable people, who in the past had made their contributions to society. It called the workhouse "a disgrace to Wales"[4] and criticised the Pwllheli Board of Guardians for deferring any decision about increasing and upgrading the staffing in consideration of the Pwllheli Union rates. The old Pwllheli workhouse building can still be seen in Ala Road, Pwllheli and it now serves as the local Health Clinic.

Until well into the 20th century, being committed to the workhouse was comparable to imprisonment in the eyes of most people for, apart from the degrading conditions, it was the denial of freedom and liberty and the separation from other family members that was most feared.

(1) cited by Thomas, David in *Hen Llongau Sir Gaernarfon*.
(2) Hyde-Hall, E ibid
(3) Report on the Borough of Nefyn, 1836.
(4) Article in 'John Bull' dated 27th August 1921.

22. VISITORS AND HOLIDAY MAKERS

As previously mentioned, during the Middle Ages when the domestic religious pilgrimage was popular and Nefyn lay at an important place on the pilgrim route to Enlli, large numbers of visitors came to Nefyn, staying within the town to rest and refresh themselves before proceeding on their way. As the regular stopping places along the pilgrim route were geared up to providing for the needs of those travelling the pilgrim route, Nefyn and other places along the way must have been the medieval equivalent of a modern holiday resort.

During this period several visitors of note came to Nefyn. On the eve of Palm Sunday 1188, Archbishop Baldwin and Archdeacon Gerald Cambrensis, stayed at Nefyn (almost certainly at the Priory of St Mary) during their tour of Wales to gain support for the Crusades. Perhaps the most spectacular Nefyn gathering of visitors of all time occurred in 1284 when Edward I held his ostentatious and costly 'Round Table' tournament to celebrate his conquest of Gwynedd, for all the famous dignitaries of Edward's kingdom were there, together with many important guests from foreign parts. Nefyn had never seen so many important visitors before; nor has it seen such a gathering since. In January 1295 Edward I again visited Nefyn, where he stayed on the nights of 12th and 13th, during his campaign to put down the Welsh uprising of 1294-5.

Later a succession of travel writers journeying through the land visited Nefyn. They recorded a vast amount of topographical, historical, geographical, antiquarian, zoological and botanical information about the regions through which they passed and the settlements they visited. Leland passed through 'Trenoven', as he called it, during his itinerary of 1536-9. After visiting Nefyn, prior to writing his Britannia in 1586, Willaim Camden observed that it was no more than a village. Thomas Pennant, who came to Nefyn in the 1770's referred to it as a small town. Fenton, visiting in 1804, reported it as "a poor straggling, miserable place....neither dignified with Town Hall or handsome church"[1].A few years later Edmund Hyde-Hall (1809-11) described it thus: "The town presents an assemblage of mean houses than is commonly met with in this part of the country, and though the houses are a good deal scattered about, they still give the impression of a considerable collected population"[2]. A visitor in 1834 was even more uncomplimentary, observing that, "the houses are irregularly built and of mean appearance, the streets are neither paved nor lighted and the inhabitants are but indifferently supplied with water"[3].

Widespread travel by land in North Wales was an option for very few prior to the second half of the 19th century. As noted in an earlier section, most roads were little more than dirt tracks, suitable only for those travelling on foot or horseback. This was especially true of Llŷn, which 18th century travellers saw as extending beyond the bounds of civilisation. Before the end of the 18th century, at certain seaside places including one or two settlements on the north-facing coastline of Wales which extends westwards towards Anglesey, sea bathing had become fashionable among some of the more affluent *visitors*. Wealthier members of English society travelled to this coast by stage coach or in their own horse-drawn carriages along the newly constructed turnpikes.

But it was the construction of the railways which resulted in the burgeoning tourist travel and which brought about the growth of seaside resorts like Llandudno, Colwyn Bay and Rhyl, following the opening of the Chester to Bangor line in 1848. Cricieth and Pwllheli also developed rapidly as holiday destinations after the opening of the Cambrian Line in 1867. As this line went no further than Pwllheli and because attempts to make Porth Dinllaen the rail terminus for Ireland repeatedly failed, Nefyn did not achieve the same early recognition as a seaside resort. A publication of 1868 said of Nefyn, "The town, which formerly was a poor fishing village, has been considerably improved of late years and has several good houses, though not one good inn. It is still irregular, straggling and rather dirty. The surrounding country is uninviting, and there are no resident gentry, on which account civilisation is very backward, and the habits of the people are extremely primitive."[4]

Despite that rather unflattering view of the town, by the 1880's the sandy beaches of Nefyn and Porth Dinllaen and the outstanding natural beauty of the region were attracting summer visitors. A directory of 1886 described Nefyn thus: "Nefyn is much frequented by visitors during the summer, having a pure, bracing atmosphere and a splendid sea. There are now some excellent lodging houses, where apartments can be had at very moderate prices. There is also a good old-fashioned hostelry, the Nanhoron Arms, nearly always full by reason of excellent accommodation and moderate tariff"[5]. In addition to the Nanhoron Arms, the directory records another hotel (Belle Vue House, a family and commercial hotel in Stryd y Ffynnon) 16 lodging houses and four lots of apartments. The entry placed in the same directory by Mrs. Evans of Plas is particularly interesting, "Commodious house in the town of Nefyn, in excellent condition, pleasantly situated and most superiorly furnished, with coach house, stabling, water and all other conveniences. Five minutes walk to the seashore. The whole may be let furnished for the summer season and would admirably answer the requirements of a good family. Terms very moderate". At this time certain more affluent city dwellers would arrive to stay in the guest houses, and a few very wealthy families travelling in their own horse-drawn carriages, would arrive in Nefyn for the entire summer to hire the kind of accommodation which Mrs. Evans of Plas offered, either bringing their servants with them or hiring servants from among the local population.

One Victorian visitor to Nefyn of more modest means was George Gissing, the Wakefield-born novelist, who 'discovered' the town in 1896, as Gwyn Neale tells in his excellent little book about Gissing's visits to North Wales. Gissing loved the town's splendid, scenic setting and in letters to a friend and to his brother he expressed his sheer delight in the place, enthusing about the fine sandy seashore, the steep cliffs and the backdrop of the mountains. He lodged at the Nanhoron Arms and, during his stay, he climbed Mynydd Gwylwyr and Garn Boduan, and walked the cliffs around Porth Nefyn and Porth Dinllaen. Gissing was visiting out of season, and apart from the beauty of the area, he was captivated by the quiet and the solitude which he was able to find there. He was obviously very conscious of the way in which Colwyn Bay had been developed from the small rural hamlet which he had seen in 1873 as a boy of 15 to the bustling, brick-built resort which he saw on his next visit in 1896. He was clearly concerned that the same fate should not befall Nefyn, for he wrote to his brother that people were already visiting Nefyn from Birmingham and he hoped that hoards of wealthy people did not discover it.

Nefyn at this time was not an easily accessible holiday destination, as Gissing noted in one of his letters. He described how he had taken the train from Caernarfon to Afon Wen, a tedious journey during which the train stopped at every station en route. At Afon Wen he was forced to change trains for the short journey on the Cambrian Line to Pwllheli. Here he had to wait for a horse-drawn coach to take him the 7 miles to Nefyn, a one shilling journey in a vehicle which he described as "ramshackle".

Gissing reported that it was not possible to purchase newspapers in the town, although the London papers could be specially ordered. In his diary he recorded that he had bought some postcards at the old Post Office, for there were a number of firms producing picture postcards of Nefyn for the tourist trade before the turn of the century.

During the period immediately prior to the First World War and between the two wars, the motor omnibus and motor car made access to the peninsula much easier, and greater numbers of people started to visit the Nefyn area for their summer holidays. As a boy during the first decade of the 20th century, John Ifor Davies remembered English visitors from the cotton towns of Lancashire and Cheshire coming to Nefyn for their holidays each August. He recalled that many of the same families had been visiting every year for more than one generation. He recounted how they helped to run the Nefyn regatta and carnival and how they were a very appreciative audience at the annual Visitors' Concert in the Madryn Hall. These visitors were people who could afford the time and the expense to take an annual holiday. At this time the guest house holiday was extremely popular and large numbers of local people took in paying guests for the entire season. In 1907 Morfa Nefyn Golf Club was established with its scenic cliff top course, and for almost 100 years it has attracted golfing enthusiasts to the area.

From the 1930's onwards some Nefyn folk built chalets or sited caravans in their gardens, and during the summer months they would move their families into this seasonal accommodation so that they could hire out their houses and cottages to English visitors. After the Second World War the annual holiday in Britain became more popular, and with the advent of holidays from work with pay, the tourist industry began to mushroom. This was the heyday of the seaside holiday in Nefyn. There were times during the 1950's to the 1970's when, at the height of the summer season, the beach of Nefyn was so crowded with family groups that it was almost impossible for late comers to stake their claim to a plot of sand large enough to erect a windshield and lay out their travel rugs. As Mr. Richard John Hughes recalls, at this time many of the houses and cottages in Nefyn would be fully booked by visitors from May to September.

In 1972 Gwynedd County Council carried out a survey of holiday accommodation. The parish of Nefyn was recorded as having 2,500 bed spaces. In Llŷn, only Abersoch, Butlin's Holiday Camp, Porthmadog and Llanystumdwy had more accommodation. Nefyn recorded a mix of accommodation, although as elsewhere on the peninsula, the emphasis was on self-catering holidays, for the guest house holiday was in decline. According to the survey, approximately three quarters of the Nefyn accommodation was in the form of caravans, cottages for hire, flats, flatlets and second homes. In addition, there was a small amount of serviced accommodation provided by guest houses, bed and breakfast providers and hotels such as the Nanhoron Arms and Caeu Capel in Nefyn and the Linksway in Morfa Nefyn. The Linksway has now closed and has recently been turned into holiday flats – a sign of the changing times!

In recent years the visitor season has lengthened, as people take more breaks throughout the year. Nowadays visitors are to be found in Nefyn, not only from Easter to September, but also during the late autumn and winter. The tourist trade, which brings much needed income into the economy of the area and which provides some seasonal employment, is still very important to Nefyn, although it also brings with it certain problems. Owing to the cheap package holiday abroad where the sun is virtually guaranteed, the domestic tourist industry has been dealt a severe blow and Nefyn has been affected, as have most other seaside resorts in Britain. Although visitors still come to Nefyn and the visiting season is now much longer, holiday-makers no longer come to the town in such great numbers as they used to do 40 or 50 years ago.

(1) Hyde-Hall, E. *A Description of Caernarvonshire* 109-11.
(2) Fenton, R. *Tours in Wales* 1804-13"
(3) Lewis, S. *A Topographical Dictionary of Wales.*
(4) The National Gazetteer of Great Britain and Ireland 1868.
(5) The 1886 Postal Directory.

23. WHAT MIGHT HAVE BEEN

As mentioned previously, during the late 18th and early 19th centuries there was a concerted effort to establish Porth Dinllaen as the mail packet station and embarkation port for Ireland. It was argued that it offered a shorter route to Dublin than its rival, Holyhead, and an intense struggle developed between the Holyhead and Porth Dinllaen factions, each of which campaigned for measures which would give their preference the edge.

One of the leading campaigners for Porth Dinllaen was W A Madocks, an Englishman who was M.P. for Boston in Lincolnshire and who owned an estate at Penmorfa. Another important member of the Porth Dinllaen faction was Colonel G A Wardle, a Caernarfonshire man and the MP for Okehampton in Devon, who owned an estate at Wern, just outside what is now the town of Porthmadog.

To make Porth Dinllaen viable as the mail packet terminus for Ireland it would be necessary to build turnpikes, along which the mail coaches could easily travel. As early as the 1770's, plans were drawn up for a route from England to Porth Dinllaen. When the Porth Dinllaen Turnpike Trust Act was passed Madocks, Wardle and others were optimistic that Porth Dinllaen would win the day.

They realised that Porth Dinllaen had one great advantage over Holyhead, namely that there would be no Menai Strait to cross. In 1806 the Porth Dinllaen Harbour Company was established and plans were drawn up to build a new 300 ft. long pier at the entrance to the bay, a basin with quays, a magnificent hotel and a town at the foot of the cliffs. The inn at Tremadoc, Madocks' newly constructed village on the route of the turnpike, was to serve as a posting station on the mail route, while another posting inn, the present Madryn Arms, was built at Chwilog by Jones Parry of Madryn.

But the improvements at Porth Dinllaen were slow to take shape. When Hyde-Hall visited in about 1810 he was disappointed with what he found. The turnpike road "was unworn by a wheel"[1] and was in danger of becoming overgrown; there was little evidence of construction work at Porth Dinllaen apart from a few carpenters laying a floor at the inn; and the old pier, which was to be reconstructed, was still a ruin. He suggested that Holyhead had nothing to worry about in its contest with Porth Dinllaen.

However, the important decision would not be made locally. In 1808, a Select Committee of the House of Commons recommended the improvement of Holyhead harbour and, in the same year, the Post Office, upon the recommendation of Thomas Telford, decided to entrust the Irish Mail to the Capel Curig Turnpike route to Bangor and a ferry across the Menai Strait to Holyhead. In 1810 another Select Committee recommended the building of a bridge across the Menai and Royal Assent was given to a Bill for the improvement of Holyhead Harbour. The Holyhead harbour improvements and the building of Telford's suspension bridge across the Menai ended Porth Dinllaen's best hopes of becoming the main terminus for Ireland.

With the coming of the railways and the probability that the Royal Mail bound for Ireland would now be carried by train, Porth Dinllaen once more made a claim to become the packet station. But which route would best suit the railway? Once again there were conflicting views among the experts. Henry Archer, an Irishman, had published plans in 1835 for a line from London to Porth Dinllaen via Oxford, Worcester and mid Wales, while George Stephenson advocated a route through Chester, along the coast to Bangor and over a new rail bridge to be built across the Menai Strait to Holyhead. Others supported a route to Orme's Bay, Llandudno, which they said was most suitable as the terminal port. In 1836 Government Commissioners received reports from two more experts, Charles Vignole, an engineer, and Captain Beaufort, hydrographer to the Royal Navy. Both favoured Porth Dinllaen, largely because of the problem of building a rail bridge across the strait to Anglesey.

In spite of these expert views and after seeking further advice, the Commissioners decided in favour of Holyhead, although the Porth Dinllaen route was shown to be both shorter in distance and quicker by steam locomotive. They took the view that a rail route through mid Wales would have necessitated the costly construction of viaducts and tunnels through the mountainous Welsh interior. Once the Chester to Holyhead line had been opened as far as Bangor in 1848, and as soon as Stephenson had built his tubular steel bridge across the Strait in 1850, the contest was well and truly over.

Still there were some local people with a vested interest in Porth Dinllaen who refused to give up the fight. In the mid 1860's proposals were put forward for a harbour of refuge at Porth Dinllaen, probably in the hope of tempting some trade away from Holyhead, but no further action was taken. In the 1870's and 1880's and right up to 1913 several different schemes were put forward for a railway line from Pwllheli to Porth Dinllaen with a branch line to Nefyn. None of these schemes got off the ground, principally for lack of investment, for the local coastal shipping trade had all but ebbed away. Finally, the outbreak of the First

World War effectively killed off all attempts to develop Porth Dinllaen into a purpose-built harbour.

So this tranquil and beautiful part of Llŷn was spared the development and exploitation which would surely have occurred if Porth Dinllaen had become the packet station for Ireland. Although we can only conjecture what might have been if the Porth Dinllaen faction had won the struggle with Holyhead, it is certain that Nefyn and its immediate environs would have been dramatically changed. Those who know and love the area round Porth Dinllaen and Nefyn are glad that it was Holyhead which won the day. The preservation of Porth Dinllaen as an unspoilt and picturesque small coastal settlement is now assured, for towards the end of the 20th century, this beautiful part of the northern coastline of Llŷn was purchased by the National Trust.

(1) Hyde-Hall *A Description of Caernarvonshire 1809-11*

24. POSTSCRIPT

What of Nefyn in the 21st century? Today Nefyn is no longer an important borough and administrative centre, and a focal point for trade and commerce. Long gone are the royal plas and the crowds of pilgrims flocking into the town. Many years ago the herring shoals ceased to appear off the coast of Llŷn and the once famous Nefyn and Porth Dinllaen herring fleets have now given way to a small number of vessels fishing for crabs, lobsters and prawns, as well as whelks for the Far Eastern market. Coasting vessels no longer call at Porth Nefyn and Porth Dinllaen, and it is over 120 years since the beaches echoed to the sounds made by shipwrights and carpenters. The quarries on the mountainsides now lie abandoned, empty and silent. Moreover, the parish's long and illustrious tradition of providing sea captains and sailors for the British merchant navy is but a fading memory, barely kept alive by the scores of inscriptions on the gravestones within the parish burial grounds. Today the vessels seen in the bay, as well as those which the Porth Dinllaen lifeboat is called out to assist, are more likely to be the leisure dinghies and speedboats of visiting holiday-makers rather than local ships.

In the 21st century, despite the influx of seasonal visitors, Nefyn retains its own unique character and it remains a very Welsh settlement where the Welsh language still thrives. The town and its immediate area, which has seen so many changes in its long, eventful history, now assume a quiet leisurely air. Relatively unchanged are the beautiful, natural sandy bays of Porth Nefyn and Porth Dinllaen, and the magnificent coastal scenery of the area, set against a superb backdrop of hills and mountains. These, and the safe accessible sandy beaches, are the things which visitors still come to the area to enjoy, just as they have done since the closing years of the Victorian era.

Although today there are no buildings in Nefyn which pre-date the middle years of the 18th century, it is possible to seek out certain names, features and images within in the town and parish which remind us of Nefyn's former glories and of its fluctuating fortunes over many centuries – if one knows where to look for them and can recognise their significance.

BIBLIOGRAPHY AND SOURCES

Key to abbreviations: TCHS Transactions of the Caernarfonshire Historical Society
CRO Caernarfon Record Office, Gwynedd Archives
NLW National Library of Wales, Aberystwyth.

1. General

1 Jones-Pierce, T., *The Old Borough of Nefyn 1355-1882* in TCHS Vol. 18 (1957)

2. Parry, Henry, Typescript copy of The History of Nefyn and District from the Henry Parry Papers CRO XM/2002/198

3. Parry, Henry, Typescript copy of More History of Nefyn and Lleyn from the Henry Parry Papers CRO XM/2002/199

4. Bassett, T. M. & Davies, B.L. (eds.), *Atlas of Caernarvonshire*, Gwynedd Rural Council (1977)

5. Dodd, A. H., *A History of Caernarvonshire*, Bridge Books, Wrexham (1968)

6. Sylvester, D., *A History of Gwynedd*, Phillimore (1983)

7. Report on the Borough of Nefyn, 1836, CRO

8. Pennant, Thomas, *A Tour in Wales 1773-6* Vol. III

9. Hyde-Hall, Edmund, *A Description of Caernarvonshire*, 1809-11.

10. Fenton, Richard, *Tours in Wales 1804-13*, a supplement to Archaeologia Cambrensis 1917.

11. Lewis, S. *A Topographical Dictionary of Wales* (1834)

12. Leland, *Itinerary in England and Wales 1536-9* Vol. III Ed. Lucy Toulmin Smith (1964)

13. Lewis, E.A., *The Boroughs of Snowdonia* (1912)

14. Morris, Tom, *Morfa Nefyn*, Gwasg Carreg Gwalch.

15. Senior, Michael, *Llŷn The Peninsula's Story*, Gwasg Carreg Gwalch (1997).

16. Various Directories for North Wales, CRO.

17. Parish Registers of Baptisms, Marriages and Burials for Nefyn, 1694-20th century CRO. a). Microfilm Reels 37 and 38
b). XPE/37/1 – 8

18. Nefyn Census Returns 1841 – 1901 CRO

19. Nefyn Tithe Schedule on microfilm, CRO

20. Memorial Inscriptions in Nefyn – Public Cemetery, CRO, Microfiche M145
St Mary's Churchyard, CRO, XM/8622
Capel y Fron graveyard, CRO XM/6254/6

St. Mair Churchyard, Morfa Nefyn CRO.
21. The Caernarfonshire Quarter Sessions Records, CRO
22. Nanhoron Rental Rolls for 1777-8 and 1878 – in private hands at Nanhoron House.

2. Early and Medieval

1. The Royal Commission on Ancient and Historic Monuments in Wales, Vol. III Caernarvonshire – West (1960)
2. Prestwich, M., *Edward I*, Guild Publishing, London (1988)
3. Soulsby, I., *The Towns of Medieval Wales*, Phillimore (1983)
4. Lloyd, J.E., *The Early History of Lleyn* in TCHS Vol. 2 (1940)
5. Jones, Bedwyr L., *Rotunda Tabula neu Dwrneiment yn Nefyn yn 1284* in TCHS Vol. 34 (1973).
6. Carr, A.D., *The Black Death in Caernarfonshire* in TCHS Vol. 61 (2000).
7. Thorpe, L., (ed) *Gerald of Wales: Journey through Wales/Description of Wales*, Penguin (1978).
8. A title deed to lands in Nefyn, dated 1st July, 1586. CRO. XD2/6986/2.

3. Maritime

1. Thomas, David, *Hen Llongau Sir Gaernarfon*, Cymdeithas Hanes Sir Gaernarfon (1952).
2. Davies, J. Ivor, *Growing Up Among Sailors*, Gwynedd Archives Service (1983).
3. Eames, Aled, *Ventures in Sail* (1987).
4. Eames, Aled, *Ships and Seamen of Gwynedd*.
5. Hughes, Henry, *Immortal Sails*, T. Stephenson & Sons, Prescot, Merseyside (1977).
6. Lewis, E.A., *The Welsh Port Books 1550-1603*.
7. Parry, Henry, Typescript copy of *Historical Smuggling, Piracy, Navigation Schools etc* in the Henry Parry Papers CRO XM/2002/141.
8. Morris, Jeff, *The History of the Porth Dinllaen Lifeboats*, Coventry (1992).
9. Jones, Ivor Wynne, *Shipwrecks of North Wales*, Landmark Publishing, Ashbourne, Derbys. (1973).
10. Parry, Henry, *Wreck and Rescue along the Coast of Wales*.
11. 'Assignment of 2 shares of a sloop called Eleanor and Jane', CRO.
13. 'Records of the Pwllheli and Nefyn Mutual Marine Insurance Societies 1861-81' CRO XM/3549/3.
14. Lloyds Shipping Registers – various years from 1811 onwards, CRO.
15. Crew Lists and Agreements for various Nefyn-owned vessels, CRO.
16. Statutory Shipping Registers CRO.
   a). For the Port of Beaumaris - 9 volumes covering 1786-1855.

b). For the Port of Pwllheli as a sub port of Beamaris 1840-44.

c). For the port of Pwllheli as a sub port of Caernarfon 1844-51.

17. Annual account of the ships registered at the Port of Pwllheli 1840-71 CRO.

18. Part of an old account book and register of ships loading slates at Ynys Cyngar Sept. 1806 – May 1808. N.L.W.

4. Agriculture, Industry and Communications

1. Dodd, A.H., *Industrial Revolution in Wales*.

2. Willaims, Deiniol, *Account of the Agrarian Conditions in Caernarvonshire during the Napoleonic Era*, TCHS Vol. 3 (1941).

3. Jones, E. G., *A Survey of the Ancient and Present State of the County of Caernarvon by William Williams of Llandygai Cantref Lleyn*, TCHS Vol. 39 (1978) pp. 133-149.

4. Jones, D.V.J., *Before Rebecca – Popular Protests in Wales* 1793-1835 Lane, London 1973.

5. Letter re exchange of Lord Newborough's land with other gentry, 1830 CRO XD2/11289.

6. Commissioners Awards of Compensation re. Enclosures in Nefyn for cottages erected on waste lands within the last 20 years. CRO. XD2/11059 – 11068.

7. Jenkins, J. Geraint, *Herring Fishing in Wales in Cymru A'r Môr* (Maritime Wales) Vol. 4 (July 1979).

8. Smylie, Mike, *The Herring Fishers Of Wales*, Welsh Heritage Series No.6, Gwasg Carreg Gwalch, Llanrwst (1998).

9. Parry's *New Guide to Wales*, 1846.

10. Letters from Nefyn shipbuilders to Lord Newborough re. possibility of logs from the estates, 1845 CRO XD2/21229 and XD2/21575.

11. Abstracts of Papers from Gwynedd Mining and Quarrying Companies Vols. 1 & 2 CRO.

12. Letter from John Hutton to Lord Newborough with prospectus of Welsh Granite Quarries at Nefyn and Rival Mountain 1864, CRO XD2/1281.

13. Lease from Lord Newborough to quarry stone on Nefyn Mountain, Jan. 1866 CRO XD2/7031.

14. Letter Book of Pistyll Quarry 1872-76 CRO X/Vaynol/2382.

15. Sale Catalogue for Moel Tŷ Gwyn Sett Quarry, property of Nefyn Syenite Granite Co. Ltd. 1881 CRO XD2/14419.

16. Accounts and Letters re. The Nevin Syenite Granite Quarry 1882-85 CRO X/Vaynol/565 and 571.

17. Letters re Pistyll Quarry 1885 CRO X/Vaynol/576 and 577.

18. Particulars re. sale of Nefyn Bay Granite Quarry 1903 CRO XM/880.
19. Pritchard, R.T., *The Turnpike Trusts of Caernarvonshire* TCHS Vol. 19 (1958).
20. Pritchard, R. T., *The Porth Dinllaen Turnpike Trust* TCHS Vol. 20 (1959).
21. Kendrick, E., Typescript notes on *Coaches and Coachmen of Lleyn* CRO XM/2002/196.
22. Kaye, David, Article from *Buses and Trolley Buses before 1919* re. buses running between Pwllheli and Nefyn CRO XD28/3418/2.
23. Elis-Williams, M., *Packet to Ireland: Porthdinllean's challenge to Holyhead*, Gwynedd Archives Service (1984).

5. Religious

1. Bowen, E. G., *The Saints of Gwynedd*, TCHS Vol 9 (1948).
2. Chitty, Mary, *The Monks on Ynys Enlli* 500AD to 1252AD.
3. Johns, C.N., *The Celtic Monasteries of North Wales*, TCHS Vol. 21 (1960).
4. Johns, C.N., *Postscript to the Celtic Monasteries of North Wales*, TCHS Vol. 23 (1962).
5. Williams, Glanmor, *The Reformation in 16th century Caernarvonshire*, TCHS Vol. 27 (1966).
6. Clarke, M.L., *Church Building and Church Restoration in Caernarvonshire during the 19th century* TCHS Vol. 22 (1961).
7. Jones, Ieuen Gwynedd, *Denominationalism in the 19th century as shown in the Religious Census of 1851*, TCHS Vol. 31 (1970).
8. 'Lease of a parcel of land called Yr Offt in Nefyn from Richard Edwards to build a chapel for the use of Protestant Dissenters called Independents 1827', Nanhoron Deeds and Documents, No 502, NLW.
9. Rees, Una, *The Cartulary of Haughmond Abbey* (a transcription of the original Latin charters), Shropshire Archaeological Society and University of Wales Press. (1985).

6. Miscellaneous

1. Thomas, P.D.G., *Parliamentary Representation of Caernarvonshire in the 18th century 1709-1749*, TCHS Vol. 19 (1958).
2. Jones-Pierce, T., *An 18th century Borough Court Book* (a transcription of the Nefyn Court Book 1756-1782), TCHS Vol. 19 (1958).
3. Flynn-Hughes, C. *The Workhouses of Caernarfonshire 1760-1914*, TCHS Vol. 7 (1946).
4. Wills of Roderick Lloyd 1728/9 (CRO XD2/541), Sir William Wynn 1754 (CRO XD/2/4332), Hugh Ellis mariner 1825 (NLW B/1825/150), Hugh Roberts mariner 1827 (NLW), John Prichard yeoman farmer1836 (NLW B/1836/161).
5. 'Removal Order of William and Catherine Hughes from Llanbeblig to

Nefyn 1819' CRO XQS/1819/46.

6. 'Correspondence re removal of Robert David, pauper, from Abererch to Nefyn 1801' CRO XQS/1801/254.

7. 'Letter from a Nefyn widow with 6 children to Lord Newborough begging for financial assistance, 1839' CRO XD2/18823.

8. 'Letter from Vicar of Nefyn to Sir Robert Williams Vaughan acknowledging receipt of £15 donation to the poor, 1844' CRO XD2/352.

9. 'Letter from George Hughes, Nefyn carrier, to Lord Newborough requesting a charitable donation as he had fallen on hard times, 1847' CRO XD2/21936.

10. Williams, H.J., *The School Board Movement in Caernarfonshire* 1870-80, TCHS Vol. 50 (1989).

11. 'Letter from Vicar of Nefyn to Lady Newborough re financial predicament of Nefyn National School, 1843' CRO XD2/20280.

12. Crimmin, P.T., 'Madocks and the Removal of the Welsh Coal Duties' TCHS Vol. 43. 1982).

13. Neale, Gwyn, *All the Days were Glorious: George Gissing in North Wales,* Gwasg Carreg Gwalch, Llanrwst (1994).

14. Bond, Roland, *Tŷ Receiver and Mursefer in Nefyn: The Story of a North Wales Dwelling Site over 400 Years* (2004), an unpublished paper.

15. 'Memorial card to mark the death of John Jones aged 13, mariner, Nefyn 1866' CRO XM/960/4.

16. 'The 1878 Nanhoron Rental Roll for Nefyn' in private hands at Nanhoron House.

17. 'Register of Deaths Pwllheli Union Workhouse 1853-1914' CRO. XG1/69.

18. 'Article in John Bull, dated 27th August 1921, about the Pwllheli Workhouse and its Board of Guardians' CRO XD28/3308.

19. National Gazetteer of Great Britain and Ireland 1868.

20. The Gwynedd County Council Survey of Holiday Accommodation 1972.

Maps and Plans

1. Map of the House and Lands belonging to John Parry in the Town and Parish of Nefyn 1777 CRO XM/7744/1/97.

2. Tithe Map of Nefyn 1838 CRO.

3. 'Chart of Porthdinlleyn and Nevyn Bay and Harbour 1747' by Lewis Morris CRO XJW/MAPS/31.

4. Plans for the Development of Porth Dinllaen 1807 by Thomas Rogers CRO XM/817.

5. O.S. Map of Nefyn specially enlarged for Land Valuation (Inland

Revenue) from the Revision of 1899 and partially revised 1911, in private hands.

6. O.S Map of Nefyn 25 ins. to 1 mile 1918, in private hands.

7. Plan of Gwylwyr Quarry Nefyn, undated, CRO XM/MAPS/1563/1.

Internet Sites

1. Mynegai Morwyr Cymru – The Welsh Mariners' Index.

2. The Commonwealth War Graves Commission Site.

3. The Porth Dinllaen Lifeboat Website.

4. The Porth Dinllaen Coastguard website.